TROUBLE IN PARADISE

A Survival Manual For Couples
Who Are Parents

TROUBLE IN PARADISE

A Survival Manual for Couples
Who Are Parents

DIANNE M. AIGAKI, M.S.

DRY CREEK PRESS
NAPA, CALIFORNIA

Aigaki, Dianne M.
    Trouble in Paradise
    A Survival Manual for Couples Who Are Parents

About the Author
    Dianne Aigaki, M.S. is a counselor and therapist with seventeen years experience in the field of individual and group counseling. She has developed a wide range of seminars and workshops that include such topics as assertiveness training, couples communication, life-planning, stress management, time management and conflict resolution. As Co-Director of "Documenting Our Lives," the national family history and folklore project, she created and facilitated a series of community events to encourage families to find connections between generations and cultures.

Library of Congress Cataloging in Publication Data
Aigaki, Dianne M., 1946-
    Trouble in paradise
      1. Parenting -- Psychological aspects. 2. Marriage--
    Psychological aspects. 3. Interpersonal communication.
    I. Title.
    HQ755.87.A43 1988   646.7'8   86-72923
    ISBN   0-941941-01-9

First Published in 1988

Dry Creek Press
PO Box 2037
Napa, California 94558

Printed in the United States of America

Illustrations by Benjamin Dann III
Cover Design and Illustration by Christina Spann

This book is my gift to

Michael and Wren

ACKNOWLEDGEMENTS

A book that deals with such a common issue as couple distress after the birth of a child could never be written without the enthusiasm and insights of many, many people. From the first days when I began to talk about creating a workbook that couples could use as a vehicle for talking and listening to each other; a book that could help smooth the transition from couplehood to parenthood, I was bombarded with words of encouragement. The question, "How's the book coming? I need a copy for my niece (or nephew or son or daughter or best friend. . .)" became a guiding force that kept me writing and interviewing past the times when I was wondering if it was <u>really</u> true that men and women needed this type of input to keep them on an even keel as they began parenting. Sometimes I wondered if I had invented the idea that new parents were suffering a lot of distress and confusion. But, stories and reflections from old friends and new acquaintances would remind me that this was a very important issue to present - and that I had a special feeling for how I wanted to do it.

So, this book was written with the advice and moral support of Barbara Morse, Randy Rand, Gretta Goldenman, Hollis and Dean Williams, Don Surplus, Christina Spann, Paula Amen-Judah, Bobb Godfrey, Gino Bostrom, Mike Sorenson, Liz and Greg Graham, Maryanna Blair and Michael, Barb and Ed Lander. My three aunts Blanche, Chatty and Margaret, my parents Bill and Betsy, my daughter Wren, my brothers David, Bill and Larry and my sister Cindy gave a special contribution of attention and family involvement. Many people put in hours of time listening and giving comments and insights, and no one ever suggested to me that it was an impossible task that was better left to someone else to start or complete. Nora-Joanne Gerber, Carolyn Furman, Barbara Beyers, Sue Tempest and Nancy Adess gave valuable suggestions with the editing, and Ben Dann put forth a vital creative effort by spending many weeks working on the illustrations. A meeting and inspiring conversation with Dr. James Hamilton gave me the "push" to remember why I had first started writing TROUBLE IN PARADISE, because of my own questions about Postpartum Depression, and his friend Pete Gillham, Sr. helped me get this manuscript on its final journey to the printer.

Several hundred men and women added their own spark to this workbook flame by sharing their stories and making me privy to "secrets" of their family history that related to couples as parents.

I sincerely thank all of these people, and I hope they are proud of their contribution to the development of this book.

PREFACE

When this book was conceived seven years ago, it followed in the wake of my own couple relationship going through rough times after the birth of my daughter. As I sought to put things in order for myself and understand the changes in our lives, I encountered hundreds of people who were trying to do the same. I felt lucky in that, as a counselor in the field of psychology, I had a framework within which to work - a structure to use as I put the pieces together. Many of the people I met felt isolated in their dilemma, blaming themselves for not being able to maintain the bond of their marriage while having and caring for a new baby. They seemed unaware of the bigger picture of "couple despair" that was all around them.

One of my first quests was to find out what had been written about changes in couple relationships after the birth of a child. As I had met scores of people with the same questions, I felt sure that there must be a body of work to which both professional and laypeople could turn for answers and clarification. After searching in the professional literature, however, I was appalled at the scarcity of material that was available on any level. The few pieces I could locate tended to appeal to the research instincts of those in the field of psychology; there were just a few volumes for the couple who might be combing the library shelves for something to ease their anxieties and put their lives back in perspective. Although it seemed to me that pregnancy and the changes it brings to couple relationships is a problem of epidemic proportions few seem to be actively addressing it.

A major part of the puzzle was the question of depression after the birth of a child. I found that many women were experiencing a sense of anxiety and depression that was peculiarly tied to the birth itself. The term Postpartum Depression was certainly not foreign to me, but I found that women seemed to dismiss this part of their lives as not being part of the problem in couple adjustments. Many who seemed to be experiencing it, by observing their behavior, denied it verbally. There was always a sense that there was something shameful about having "postpartum blues," - that it had serious implications for motherhood; that it called into question the commitment and joy that should go with having a child. This part of the puzzle was highlighted as women who were interviewed in one time period and denied being depressed or having feelings of anxiety after birth, called me several years later to say, "I want you to know that when you talked about that possibility it frightened me. I couldn't stand to hear you describing something that I was feeling so acutely. I couldn't admit it then, but now I can - yes, I was depressed at that time and I couldn't say it and I didn't know where to turn for help. I thought it was my fault."

Searching for information for myself, friends and strangers who had heard about my interests, I became part of another process - the development of "Documenting Our Lives," a family history and folklore project in Northern California. This unique project creates community programs to encourage community members to share information between generations about every type of life transition. My interest in "Documenting Our Lives" came from my desire to ask people of all ages and situations, "How did your life change after you had a baby?" I felt sure that if people who were nineteen or ninety and every age in between would give me that slice of their life, I could write a book that would give hope, perspective and information to those waiting in the wings.

And they did. Men and women were eager to respond in writing and on video and in casual conversation about how the time of pregnancy and new parenthood had affected their lives - especially their life as a couple. It was not unusual for someone to call me at home and say, "I heard you are writing a book about staying together as a couple after you have a baby. I'd like to tell you my story." At parties and meetings, men and women would readily tell me their stories of courage, frustration and disillusionment as they talked about impending separations and divorces. Not all stories were sad - many told of advice passed on to them by parents and grandparents and neighbors. Many had worked out their own fascinating perspectives over many years of living. It was common for a virtual stranger to ask me, "Did you include a chapter about _____ in your book?" If I hadn't, I did.

A few times over the years I was given, it seemed quite through serendipity, a chance to talk to someone who was concerned about these basic issues and who had information far beyond what I had been able to discover in my own search. One of these people was Dr. James A. Hamilton, an expert on Postpartum Depression from San Francisco. In a several hour conversation, he enlightened me as to the statistical incidence of this problem among women and its medical basis. His work since the early 1960's corroborated all of the stories that I had already heard from men and women seeking their own answers. His insights and research in regard to treatment answered compelling questions for me that had been left dangling for many years. Through his sharing of knowledge, I saw yet again how crucial these facts and stories are in the healing of men's and women's perceptions about their lives and their roles as new parents.

As they encouraged me to work on this manual, all of these people changed and enriched my life. There have been extra benefits I could not have predicted. With the gift of hearing the stories of young and old about the transition from couplehood to parenthood, I have been able to pass on these same tales to the next listener. I believe that, through being a privileged courier, I have left many with hope for a future with their partner when they had begun to doubt.

As I wrote, I realized that what I wanted to do in this book was not only to focus on answering basic questions, but also to offer a format to enable couples to derive answers that are unique to them. For every couple will have a slightly different challenge, and the truth of the matter is that *their* closeness and healing will develop from within as they open their ears and hearts to *each other's* stories and to the real information about how others go through this time of transition. For myself, I have grown in understanding and compassion for the struggles of women, men and children as they strive to keep their dreams of a family together. And TROUBLE IN PARADISE has allowed me the time and the vision and the information to heal my own family relationships. Indeed, I sometimes forget, that was what sent me off on this quest seven years ago.

This is my story, too, and it's why I wrote this book.

DEDICATION

David, Sheryl and Skylar
and
Hollis, Dean and Blair
Elizabeth, Billy and Leigh
Don, Lynne and Lili
Janice, Alan and Danielle
Gretta, Greg and Casey
Arlene, Mike, Lindsey and Julia
Mark, Debbie and Laurel
Julie, Chips and Luke
Paul, Pam, Kevin and Denali
Jeff, Susan and Marita
Steve, Jean and Breeze
Jeffrey, Patti and Emily
Francisco, Rosa and Sophia
Todd, Katie and Max
Bob, Barbara and Ryan
Kit, Michael and Lydie
Barbara, Martin, Frank, and Rue
David, Nancy and Claire
Kris, Jim and Adam
Busy, Baird and Alana
Nancy, Jack and Anne
Virginia, Greg and Alice
Sandy, Don, Jennifer and Kellee
David, Beth and Tai
John, Rebecca and Maria

TABLE OF CONTENTS

INTRODUCTION

Pregnancy and new parenthood are experiences we are all involved in one way or another. Even if we don't have children ourselves, we can't escape the interweaving that happens when our friends and neighbors make this decision. And, in fact, we may still be spending days and nights musing about the circumstances that brought our own parents together and those that may have pushed them apart. It behooves us to understand what we and our fellow humans are thinking and feeling during this period of time. Young and old alike need to share in the reality of this life passage and, in the process, defuse the emotional time bomb that this transition sometimes becomes.

ONE THING IS CERTAIN, HAVING A BABY CAN BE THE LIGHTEST, HAPPIEST POINT OF YOUR LIFE; OR DESPITE YOUR PREPARATION, MOTIVATION OR MENTAL HEALTH, IT CAN BE AN EXPERIENCE SO TRYING THAT IT CREATES AN AIR OF EXHAUSTION IN A FAMILY THAT ONLY SEPARATION CAN ALLEVIATE. COUPLES WHO LOVE EACH OTHER DEARLY AND TREASURE THEIR NEW CHILD CAN NEVERTHELESS BE THROWN INTO A WHIRLWIND OF INDECISION AND ANTAGONISM AS THEY ADJUST TO THE ROLE OF BEING PARENTS.

HOW DO PEOPLE GO THROUGH THIS TRANSITION? WHAT DO THEY LEARN? WHAT QUESTIONS DO THEY ASK? AND, IN THE FINAL ANALYSIS, HOW CAN THEY SERVE AS RESOURCES FOR THE MANY OTHERS WHO WILL PASS THROUGH A VERY SIMILAR TRANSITION - FROM COUPLEHOOD TO PARENTHOOD?

As a beginning, many are relieved to know that difficulties during this transition are common. Furthermore, those who have had revitalizing experiences need to share these stories of personal and couple triumph and growth. These people are key resources who can, if they will, pass on solutions and support for their friends and neighbors who will follow. They have new perspectives and ideas for enhanced communication for those who are struggling.

As our society grows further and further away from parents and grandparents playing the traditional role of guides for the younger generations, there is a serious gap in the information chain. This information isn't just about the trivialities of life. It doesn't even have to do with how it felt to be the first person on the block with a color television or the first family in town to own a car. These stories provide the spice of life, but there are other tales that are the meat. **How have you learned to be close to your family and friends? How have you become the person you are today? What events and decisions led you through your life? What do you cherish in your history? What do you regret? What do you wish someone had told you? What can you tell us about succeeding as parents and as a couple?**

THIS IS A TIME OF CHANGE

Pregnancy and new parenthood are extremely intense times of transition for almost everyone who experiences them, yet these times of change are relatively little understood. We can all remember people telling us that having a baby would change our lives; few enter into parenthood so naively as to think that this wouldn't be so. But, the high numbers of people who divorce or separate after the birth of a child would indicate that few of us truly comprehend the extent and variety of changes that parenthood will bring, and just how they will impact all areas of our lives.

As families grow up and move apart, there are fewer family members nearby to serve as resources for this type of information. It's not as if our friends don't try to help us understand; but having your peers be your main resource is a little like being on a team without a coach. Everyone is working together, but no one may have the experience or the next level of information that will make things clearer and go more easily. With no reference point for success or failure - no news on feelings and conflicts and solutions from other generations - new parents are more likely to bitterly blame themselves or their partners for the difficulties that arise while they attempt to adjust to new life roles and attitudes.

A large percentage of couples separate or divorce within two years after the birth of their first child. For many there is not only a severe strain on their couple relationship, but also a breach in their relations with their parents, friends and   children. Futhermore, it doesn't exempt them as as individuals.

The time of transition may be so confusing and disturbing that individuals and couples are left with a residue of frustration that causes direct problems in other areas of their lives, too. Both men and women routinely miss work and function poorly in their jobs due to relationship stress. For many of these people, the stresses are arising concurrently with the birth of a child.

New parents must deal with stresses that are unique to partnerships, and which carry their own brand of confusion and volatility. As we move from couplehood to parenthood, the stakes change and issues emerge in a different light. Have you ever noticed how problems that were just different points of view before marrying or before having a child can become insurmountable, non-negotiable obstacles afterwards? Have you noticed how an issue that might have been resolved through discussion or even argument before, can become a free-for-all, a stand-off or a symbol of alienation after?

What is happening here? What is the process that couples are going through in such a short period of time that they seemingly transform from partners looking at the future with an expectant eye, to wary strangers afraid of what the next disagreement will bring to their tenuous circumstances? Is this happening because the partners have changed so drastically? Is it because they are finally seeing the truth of their individual differences and inabilities to handle conflict and compromise? Is it because they fooled themselves about the viability of their relationship from the beginning? Or is it possible that the unique stresses and expectations of couplehood and parenthood are requiring a new set of communication skills and problem-solving techniques and a commitment to understanding on a much deeper level?

These are some of the interpersonal questions that come naturally to the forefront. Other questions that speak to these same blocks in handling "new parenting" have to do with the physiological changes that new mothers go through after the birth. Is it possible that the hormonal/biological stresses of birth and postpartum recovery are hampering the ability to marshall necessary resources toward couple relationship solutions? Just as communication gaps must be taken seriously, so it is essential to seriously consider the physiological state of the new mother and how that may be affecting her on a psychological level as well as emotional level. These issues may be prevalent in our society, but are not always understood by new parents.

"I wonder why my sister and brother always blamed me when our parents got divorced?"

Parents are not the only ones to suffer from a lack of understanding about the issues of pregnancy and new parenthood. Older children in the family also feel the anxieties and the attempts to regain physical and emotional equilibrium. They see the changes that their parents go through after the birth of a new baby or while caring for a young child. These brothers and sisters may hold the new sibling responsible for the change in family life and these "accusations" may color a lifetime of family interaction.

3

Maryanne talked with a great deal of sorrow about her homelife as she was growing up. Her older sister had beaten her as a child and had been a constant source of fear and anxiety. Maryanne could never understand why her parents didn't step in and help her out. Only when they were adults could Maryanne's sister explain her hatred of Maryanne.

She said that when Maryanne was born their mother had been very depressed and the other children in the family were sent to live with relatives for a year. Their father had to work two jobs to pay for the mother's medical bills and send financial support to the relatives who had "adopted" the older children. The mother was eventually able to care for her family again, but not before both parents were emotionally and financially drained as a result of the events that followed Maryanne's birth. They divorced two years later and never recovered their sense of home and warmth as a family. The elder sister associated Maryanne with the disruption of the family and the changes in her mother and it was only when she could tell her the feelings from the perspective of adulthood that the relationship began to heal.

As I talked with men and women about their families, and their memories, I heard many stories about the effect of a birth on the sense of security and esteem of the other children. Many tales were so extreme and puzzling that, for me, they cast a new light on the theory of "sibling rivalry." The message that came through loud and clear was not "This is how my parents showered more affection on my new brother or sister and I was jealous," but rather: "This is how I saw my parents change after the baby was born. My mother became depressed, my father became angry, this baby brought turmoil into our lives - my parents' relationship changed drastically and we were part of it." There is no lack of such stories of familial stress in our society. **The question is, when faced with such a change in behaviors and roles, when lives are not following the expected happy script, what is the next step?**

SOME MAY THINK IT'S TIME TO CALL IT OFF. I THINK IT'S TIME TO TRUST THOSE INITIAL FEELINGS AND LOOK AT THE RELATIONSHIP FROM A NEW VANTAGE POINT. IT'S TIME TO BREAK THROUGH THE BARRIERS AND AFFIRM THE FEELINGS AND IDEALS THAT FIRST BROUGHT YOU TOGETHER AS A COUPLE AND ENCOURAGED YOU TO THINK THAT YOU COULD BE PARENTS AND LOVING PARTNERS FOR A LIFETIME RELATIONSHIP.

FOR OUR PURPOSES, WE WILL ASSUME THAT IF YOU ARE HAVING DIFFICULTY IN YOUR RELATIONSHIP, YOU HAVE:

1) TRIED TO WORK OUT THE ISSUES

2) TRIED TO UNDERSTAND YOUR OWN NEEDS AND DESIRES

3) TRIED TO UNDERSTAND THE PERSPECTIVE OF YOUR PARTNER

4) TRIED TO ARRIVE AT A WORKABLE SOLUTION

Someone else looking at the situation might feel that you have done none of the above. If you have become demoralized, you may even doubt the value of your intentions in resolving the conflicts. Yet, be assured that almost everyone who is faced with a life challenge brings to it all of the forces they can muster to reduce the turmoil and bring equilibrium back into their lives.

The problem is that we don't always have an extensive range of ideas for how to do this. We aren't always creative with our problem-solving, and we can't always work past the short-term to prepare for the long-range. We don't always recognize that life is full of common transitions and that thousands of people have gone before us and have tried out scores of solutions. We usually don't think we can ask them to share with us the information that they have gathered and which may have been passed on to them.

And, if that isn't enough, we can't always identify what we want or need. And we don't always feel good enough about our partner at any one point in time to see his or her side of the issue.

SO, WE BRING TO THE CONFLICT ALL OF THE STRATEGIES THAT WE CAN THINK OF, AND STILL WE FALL SHORT. WHEN THIS HAPPENS, IT IS IMPORTANT TO EXAMINE OUR MODES OF TALKING AND LISTENING. WE NEED TO EVALUATE OUR WAYS OF PROBLEM-SOLVING AND PERHAPS DEVELOP NEW SKILLS IN THESE AREAS. WE MAY NEED TO LOOK AROUND US A BIT MORE TO LEARN FROM OTHERS, AND WE MAY NEED TO ADOPT A GREATER SENSE OF COMPASSION FOR OURSELVES AS WE STRUGGLE WITH NEW ROLES, FEELINGS AND IDEAS.

5

TROUBLE IN PARADISE is composed of exercises that will encourage you to take into account the new expectations, goals, fears and dreams that come with being a parent. It will also help you to see your own and your family history and to understand how these histories have influenced you as an adult, as part of a couple and as a parent. And, it will give you very real information about some of the physiological and psychological changes that new parents experience that are essential to understand.

These exercises address areas of conflict and decision-making that men and women routinely face as they move through the different stages of their lives. In some ways, how you are affected by being a parent is not much different from how you are affected by any major life event. It depends on your experiences growing up, the messages you have been given by parents and grandparents, and what you learn by observing the world around you. In short, the impact of problems and transitions for each of us is filtered by our individual differences and unique life quests and directions. But, it is also true that the internal changes of pregnancy and childbirth and your reactions to these events may call forth a way of "dealing with problems " or "not dealing with problems " that is unlike any other way you can remember acting in the past or will act in the future.

This manual does not speak to all issues, but rather provides a format for discussion and reflection. It is hoped that this format will give you techniques for communication you can use throughout your lifetime. The manual will help you explore issues in such a way as to remove the spectre of blame and guilt that often accompanies new parenting. Doing the proposed exercises will encourage an attitude of mutual respect and understanding for the very real challenges that men and women face as they grow in their own lives while trying to develop stable, meaningful relationships.

THIS MANUAL EVOLVED FROM THE BELIEF THAT THE PROBLEM LIES NOT WITH THE INDIVIDUAL OR THE COUPLE, BUT IN FAULTY UNDERSTANDING OF THE ISSUES AND THEIR ORIGINS. ALL PROBLEMS CAN BE SEEN FROM MANY PERSPECTIVES; OUR BEST WILL COME FROM RECOGNIZING AND UNDERSTANDING THE ATTITUDES WITH WHICH WE APPROACH THE SOLUTIONS.

WE CAN TAKE THIS UNDERSTANDING EVEN ONE STEP FURTHER BY CHOOSING, AS PARTNERS, TO SHARE THIS KEY INFORMATION ABOUT HOW OUR ATTITUDES HAVE BEEN FORMED AND HOW THEY ARE INFLUENCING OUR CURRENT LIFE DIRECTIONS, FEELINGS AND DECISIONS.

TAKE THE TIME TO REFLECT SERIOUSLY ON THESE EXERCISES

Strengthening (or creating) intimacy with your partner is serious business! You deserve to give yourself the time to do it well. By "taking this seriously," I don't mean to suggest an approach that is "doom-saying" or that feels like another heavy weight added to what may already seem to be quite a burden of time commitment and responsibility. I am talking about getting closer rather than further apart.

If you are reading this manual with your partner, find the time to be together (if at all possible) to work through these exercises. Some are long, many are very short. Go somewhere, away from family, friends and responsibilities and relax while reflecting on (and sharing) the very important information that this manual will encourage you to examine. **This is the time to get a babysitter for a few hours and spend time alone.**

I recommend choosing a specific day of the week (i.e. every Tuesday night from 6:30 to 8:30) that you adhere to week after week. Go to a place with pleasant surroundings where you can sit together and remember what it is like to have a common goal. For indeed, you are experiencing a very common life transition, and even if it seems like a struggle, you are both on the same side.

"I want to tell you what I was thinking when we wrote those stories about our families."

How long it takes to do these exercises doesn't matter. You might find that two hours is the time it takes to complete an exercise and talk about it. Two hours, four hours or two weeks - these pages will start a pattern of reflection and sharing that will last a lifetime and be passed on to others. **Relationships of love and intimacy beg for long-term results. Take as long as you need to make these results happen.**

This manual is not meant to be a total course in communication skills or problem-solving. The exercises are building blocks that will create a foundation and structure over a lifetime. They will give you clues to begin to understand the difficulties you are having and how you can develop plans for achieving a new and very necessary perspective.

FOLLOW THE DIRECTIONS FOR EACH OF THE EXERCISES.
WORK ON THEM SEPARATELY, AND THEN SHARE THE INFORMATION WITH YOUR
PARTNER

These exercises were designed to be enjoyable to complete, but they are not games. They are "tried and true" techniques used by business consultants, teachers and counselors to create a climate for communication.

If they feel stilted, forced or unnatural in the beginning, continue anyway. It is very common to want to dismiss the larger picture because of difficulty in the initial stages. Feelings of embarrassment or discomfort will quickly disappear as you become familiar with the communication techniques and see the results.

This manual will give you practice in asking questions of yourself and your partner. It does not have the answers, but it will lead you back through your life and that of your family and help make important connections with your present day attitudes and behaviors. It will assist you in defining your goals, hopes and dreams for the future. **You will find that the "content" of the answer is often not as important as the fact that you have become part of an information and feeling exchange with your partner.**

Always remember that your partner is like you. He or she is searching for the reasons behind events that may well be contributing to the difficulties or the strengths of the partnership. You will each be stretching yourselves to complete each exercise on your own. It will take courage, hope and imagination to fill in the blanks and relax with the information that you gather. Try to adopt an attitude of interest, speculation and compassion for both yourself and your partner as you reflect on what you are thinking, feeling and learning.

Once you have looked at your own story, sharing these findings takes another level of courage and commitment, and you will need to practice trust in each other to make it work. These exercises will provide a framework for building that trust as you learn more about yourself and your partner and come to terms with the dynamics of the relationship and explore what you both envision for the future.

THE RESOLUTION OF CONFLICTS WILL FOLLOW NATURALLY FROM THE HEARTFELT COMMUNICATION OF HOPES AND DREAMS, AND FEARS AND HISTORIES.

WHAT IF I'M NOT A COUPLE ANYMORE, AND I'M WORKING ON THESE EXERCISES ALONE?

When these chapters were developed, the hope was that couples would be sitting down together and working through the exercises, then sharing the information. Unfortunately, the truth of the matter is that many people will be working alone - trying to understand what happened in their couple relationship, so that they can be better prepared for the next one. They will be working to ease their own pain and to gain personal insight and strength that goes beyond the coupling issues.

For the many men and women that are included in this group of solo readers, I would ask that you not be dismayed by the instructions that frequently guide the manual user to share thoughts and reflections with their partner. Instead, turn to friends, family, neighbors and community groups to talk about these issues and the feelings they provoke in you. Perhaps, a circle of men or women friends could use this manual to inspire conversation about relationships in general. Single parents and parents-to-be can all benefit from the passing on of these types of information and histories. Many couples who use this manual will be part of a burgeoning group of parents who have sought out alternative ways of becoming a family. There are many men working together as partners and women as partners who are striving hard to create couple relationships and family atmospheres that will provide comfort and happiness to all the family members. This manual is for them, too.

FOR PROFESSIONALS WHO USE THIS BOOK IN COUNSELING

Coming to this project via my own experience as a professional counselor, I created these exercises with the expectation that professionals in the helping fields could benefit from using this book as an adjunct to their own counseling methods. There is ample room for therapist input and guidance, and the format lends itself well to small group and workshop sessions. It may also be used as a training manual to stimulate student discussion of couple and family counseling techniques.

IS THIS MANUAL THE SAME AS BEING IN THERAPY?

TROUBLE IN PARADISE was not designed to be used as a substitute for therapy or counseling. It is meant to help you begin to enhance your ability to understand yourself and open up to your partner, so that relationship rifts will come to the surface and be healed. The work you do here may provide enough momentum on its own for you to be able to relax and get on with the excitement and joy of your life. Or, it may give you only a glimpse of how further work can help you clarify your feelings and life directions. It may even highlight serious gaps that will move you to seek other assistance and other conclusions.

Because these exercises are similar to what you might experience in some forms of therapy, you may find that you have even deeper thoughts, feelings and experiences to explore. This exploration could continue with a professional counselor who is trained to assist individuals, couples and families to move through times of crisis to more stability and satisfaction. Often people wonder how a counselor could help with a problem that the man or woman or couple sees as being uniquely their own. The answer is that counselors have been educated to help others to see themselves and their situations more clearly. Through their training and experience, they have usually acquired techniques that can provide valuable information and direction. Just as your skills may be in the area of computers or truck driving or sales, their skills are in communication and psychological insight. They study the dynamics of relationships and understand how people learn to change areas of conflict in their lives. Their job is to listen and possibly suggest action and action alternatives.

If you decide that seeing a professional counselor would be a good next step for you, their job will be easier and counseling will proceed more quickly if you have an idea beforehand of what your concerns may be. TROUBLE IN PARADISE will help you see some of the areas on which you would like to concentrate.

Good luck!

CHAPTER ONE

UNDERSTANDING

TALK TO ME - LISTEN TO ME

After each exercise in this manual, take TWENTY minutes to talk while your partner listens. Your partner will have twenty minutes to talk when you are through. Listening works best, of course, when no one is interrupting! Dialogue will take place when both parties have had their chance at center stage.

notes/thoughts/ideas
talk to. . .
ask about. . .

At first, twenty minutes to talk or to listen can seem like forever. If you aren't used to having someone's undivided attention, it may be an unnerving experience. If you aren't used to giving someone your undivided attention, you might feel like jumping out of your seat (or yawning, or reading the newspaper, or washing the dishes, or. . .).

Try to remember that you are telling about and listening to vital information that has to do with an important person in your life. From these stories and reflections you will gain valuable insights about how struggles with life issues have formed, directed and challenged you as partners. Hopes and fears and dreams are the stuff of life, and exchanging these confidences will build trust and reassurance in your relationship and your ability to grow as friends and survive the "hard times."

Communication does not stop with your partner, however. It is important to develop a sense of how you can go beyond your couple relationship for this same type of information and insight about the world. Whenever possible, turn to a person of another generation for clues as to how they handled similar life passages. Expand your perspective by listening and sharing with them. Imagine the viewpoint that a ninety-five year old man or woman can offer when they talk about how their life changed when they had a child seventy years before!

SABOTAGE BETWEEN PERFECTLY REASONABLE PEOPLE

Direct communication isn't always easy. Men and women establish entire careers based on helping families, corporations, and groups large and small learn how to talk and how to listen. Below are some of the concepts that they have found to be important to consider. For instance, despite the fact that you may want to improve your relationship with your partner and come to understand the issues which are causing you difficulty, you may unconsciously try to sabotage the communication efforts by doing any one of a number of things:

1- laughing at the communication "rules"
    Initial embarrassment or anxiety might cause you to make light of this system for talking and

listening to each other. It's fairly common for men and women (and children) to laugh at things that are actually serious to them, and thereby attempt to dilute the importance of the information in their lives. This is also a technique that covers up the "real" impact that the words are having on their feelings - feelings they may never have faced alone <u>or</u> with a partner.

2- interrupting

Fear, inconsideration and general lack of awareness can cause us to interrupt our partners as they tell us about important parts of their lives. If you are an interrupter, this behavior will, over a period of time, make the teller less interested in sharing their story with you. In fact, it will cause bitterness and anger because you seem unwilling to respect the views of your mate, despite your common concerns and common goals for happiness.

3- showing disinterest

Some men and women are so unused to listening to their partners they will actually get up and walk away when the speaker is in the middle of a sentence. They may fall asleep at times of crucial communication. They may read the paper or cook dinner or start to mow the lawn while their partner is earnestly attempting to reveal their innermost self. Disinterest can come from many sources, but the only result will be that the teller will give up and withdraw if you cannot find a reason for listening - and listening with care to what they have to say.

4- holding back

"Not being able" to sincerely say what is on your mind can come from anxiety, fear of not being taken seriously, or a feeling that you don't have adequate words for communicating. Do you need to tell all? Some issues, some thoughts, and some feelings may seem "too private" or "too hot to handle." You may wish to keep these to yourself for the time being. Partners also need to grant each other the right to private inner lives with the acknowledgement that more sharing will strengthen the bond of the relationship. And indeed, this is the goal.

IF YOU NOTICE THESE ACTS OF SABOTAGE HAPPENING, QUICKLY AFFIRM YOUR DESIRE TO TELL AND LISTEN, AND <u>MOVE ON</u>. ADDRESS YOUR FEELINGS WITH A SIMPLE STATEMENT SUCH AS, "I'M LAUGHING, BUT IT'S BECAUSE I'M NERVOUS ABOUT WHAT YOU'RE SAYING. . ." DO BETTER THE NEXT TIME.

PART OF YOU MAY WISH TO SABOTAGE, BUT ANOTHER PART WISHES TO JOIN FORCES WITH YOUR PARTNER IN LEARNING AND LOVING. PRACTICE BRINGING THAT ASPECT OF YOURSELF TO THE FOREFRONT AND LETTING THE "SABOTEUR" RETREAT TO THE SHADOWS.

GETTING THE MESSAGE ACROSS

WHAT IS HEARD AND UNDERSTOOD CAN REDUCE ALIENATION, FEAR AND FRUSTRATION.
WHAT IS HIDDEN CAN CREATE ALIENATION, FEAR AND FRUSTRATION.

One person in a relationship is often more verbal than the other. This person may be more comfortable expressing feelings, analyzing actions, questioning motives, etc. But this person is not necessarily "right" just because they have the words to get the message across. They may have grown up in a family where "talking" came easily. They may have put more effort into understanding the issues and translating this understanding into words. Or, they may have merely developed a skill that allows them to "talk over and around" what is really the issue at hand.

IF YOU ARE THE MORE VERBAL PERSON
You have a special challenge - not to overpower your partner with words, but to respect his or her feelings and thoughts, even though they are not being expressed in your style. Your challenge is to listen carefully for the messages between the lines and be careful to avoid overlaying your own words and interpretations without first checking out the accuracy of these perceptions with your partner.

It doesn't really matter how clearly you see the issues, if you can't talk about them in a way that allows your partner to be comfortable with and open to the information. Both parties need to feel safe and respected if they are to put their perspectives forward without fear or hesitation.

The partner who does not express him/herself as clearly or as easily in words may not have a poorer understanding of the issues, the dynamics of the interaction or their own feelings. Their style is simply different and could have evolved from growing up in a family where people did not talk about their ideas or perceptions of the world. They may have been discouraged in the past by an intimidating partner, may never have learned verbal commmunication skills, or may never have had the practice to make it flow easily. They may not value the role of "talker," seeing it as frivolous

15

posturing but being glad to be a "listener." Whatever the reason, this person can be "run over" by the talker, and can neglect to participate in the true workings of the partnership by refusing to come forward and speak his or her piece.

IF YOU ARE THE LESS VERBAL PERSON

Your challenge is to nurture your skill in talking so that your partner has the chance to know you and gain vaulable feedback from your ideas and insights. Your challenge is to avoid "hiding out" with your thoughts and come forward even if you do not have just the "right words at the right time."

"Don't leave, I'm listening now. I really am. Don't let all of my talking get in the way. Please start again. I'm listening!"

THE SKILLS OF TALKING AND LISTENING TAKE TIME TO DEVELOP. BY FINE-TUNING THIS ART OF COMMUNICATION, YOU WILL BE PROVIDING YOUR PARTNER WITH HIS OR HER BEST CHANCE TO UNDERSTAND WHAT IS IMPORTANT TO YOU. AND YOU WILL BE PROVIDING A RARE AND PRICELESS GIFT IN EXCHANGE - THE FEEDBACK THAT ONLY A DEVOTED FRIEND AND INTIMATE COMPANION WILL GIVE ABOUT ACTIONS AND REACTIONS TO THE WORLD.

WE'RE BOTH ON THE SAME SIDE

notes/thoughts/ideas
talk to. . .
ask about. . .

It's common for new parents to find themselves on opposite sides of a seemingly unresolvable issue. The stakes may appear to be critical. Winning or losing can be symbolic or may have real significance in terms of how you will conduct your daily lives. Conflicts which were dealt with as a matter of course before the arrival of the child may now loom as frightening symbols of incompatibility and inflexibility.

Carla and Ryan brought high hopes for compatibility into their marriage. They had been together since high school, went to the same college, and then moved away to a small town when Ryan got a job with a manufacturing firm. Over the years of their courtship, they seldom argued, and when they did, they found it was easy to compromise and let the incident pass.

Both Carla and Ryan were looking forward to the birth of their child. When the baby arrived, they were settled in a new home with money in the bank and plans for the future. When the change came, it didn't happen overnight, but neither of them could put their finger on what had precipitated it. They went from being a happy, argument-free household to a home edged with tension. The fights they had did not seem to be about anything monumental, but somehow they ended with harsh words that had never been spoken before.

Money had not been an issue in the past, but now they had frequent disagreements about how to spend it, and how much they needed to have to be "on the safe side." Dividing up housework, what to do about childcare, how much time to spend with friends - all of these issues took their toll on these new parents. They were left with a sense of uneasiness about their apparent inability to still "like each other."

After three months of tension, Carla and Ryan went to a community workshop for new parents. There they found that they weren't alone - that the problems they were having were fairly common, and that their neighbors had lots of ideas they could try out before giving up.

" I can't believe the fights we get in over the most petty things! It's driving me crazy!"

17

Carla and Ryan found that the new game of parenthood had a different set of rules and directions than they were used to. They had to learn to listen to each other's needs and expectations with "new ears" because they were each experiencing a set of emotions that hadn't been present during their courtship and early marriage.

As they continued to talk with people in the community workshop, they began to recognize new fears concerning parenting. They eventually discovered that talking about the issues and trying to convince each other of the validity of their viewpoint was not as important as telling about their histories and families and describing their feelings. The new perspectives they were developing as they did so turned out to contain more vital information than the topics that had provided an endless battleground during the previous months.

They gained information through the couple workshops that they hadn't found anywhere else - information about real people moving through real life transitions, and not so easily. Ryan was moved to tears hearing some of the mothers talk about "baby blues" and their fear of never feeling "like themselves" again. He looked at Carla's anxieties with a new understanding and found that he could offer real support to her and the other couples when they needed it.

Through this type of communication, this calm talking and listening, Carla and Ryan defused the sense of panic at not reaching agreement or compromise. They were no longer the "model couple," but instead two adults who had grown to recognize dissimilarities as part of the package of human interaction. Once they left behind the need never to be seen with a conflict, they were able to talk more openly with friends about their difficulties and seek out others for insight and advice.

NOT EVERY ISSUE CAN BE AGREED UPON, BUT ALL CAN BE UNDERSTOOD IN TERMS OF THE IMPORTANCE FOR THE PEOPLE INVOLVED. IT IS TO YOUR MUTUAL BENEFIT THAT YOU LISTEN TO YOUR PARTNER'S NEEDS, EXPECTATIONS, FEARS, HISTORY AND ASPIRATIONS, FOR THEY ARE PROFOUNDLY AFFECTING YOUR OWN LIFE. IT IS TO YOUR MUTUAL BENEFIT TO REALIZE THAT YOU ARE BOTH ON THE SAME SIDE IN THIS LIFE TRANSITION - TRYING TO STAY TOGETHER AS A FAMILY AND BE CLOSER AS A COUPLE.

ON THE SAME SIDE

It's probably pretty obvious to you what issues you <u>don't</u> agree on. It's probably ringing clear as a bell where you have differences, so we won't dwell on those. Instead, it's time to remember where you do agree - the parts of your life and the shared values where you are both on the same side and can support each other. In the turmoil of adjusting to being a couple or being new parents, the grounds of commonality can sometimes get obscured by emphasis on relationship brush fires.

FILL OUT THE FOLLOWING CHART
Take the time to think about where you <u>do</u> agree, where you feel confident
that you are both working toward the same goals

This is how we work well together:

1.

2.

3.

**These are the areas in which we both have concerns
and are trying to find solutions:**

1.

2.

3.

In terms of our lives now, we both want to:

1.

2.

3.

In terms of our life goals, we both believe in:

1.

2.

3.

**In what other areas of your life, do you find common ground
as partners and as parents?**

1.

2.

3.

SHARE YOUR RESPONSES WITH YOUR PARTNER

20

TEN MYTHS ABOUT COUPLES

Every aspect of society and human relations carries with it a whole collection of myths that we often incorporate into our beliefs without realizing it. There are myths about money, myths about in-laws and myths about work. Marriage partnerships and parenting are by no means immune to this phenomenon!

Exposing the personal "myths" that keep you and your partner confused or angry is an important step in releasing their ability to subtly direct your life. Peel back the myths, like you would peel back the layers of an onion!

The chart on the following page lists ten famous myths about life and love.

    1. **Read through** the list of myths.

    2. **Check** those that seem to describe you.

    3. **Check** those that remind you of your parents.

    4. **Check** those that describe a couple you know well.

    5. **Doublecheck** those myths that are particularly disturbing to you, either because they sound all too familiar, or evoke a strong emotional response.

    6. **Triple check** those that prompted you to say, "Yes, but this really isn't a myth, this is true for me (or them)."

You'll notice that there are myths scattered throughout this manual. Each one has a short section of questions for you to consider and answer, and share with your partner.

TEN MYTHS ABOUT COUPLES

	me	my parents	a couple I know	disturbing to me	"this is true!"
Myth 1 - **You always hurt the one you love.**					
Myth 2 - **Everyone in my family gets divorced. I'm just like them.**					
Myth 3 - **I'm (we're) waiting until we have the time to deal with this.**					
Myth 4 - **Sometimes people get along so well that they don't have any excitement or mystery left in their relationship.**					
Myth 5 - **I need a crisis to motivate me.**					
Myth 6 - **Working on a relationship is just that - too much work.**					
Myth 7 - **I (we) have already talked about this, tried to figure it out, done everything I (we) can. It's hopeless.**					
Myth 8 - **I can't get any cooperation.**					
Myth 9 - **I (he/she) always go back to doing things the same way.**					
Myth 10 -**This time of transition will never end.**					

MYTH NUMBER ONE
YOU ALWAYS HURT THE ONE YOU LOVE

This is a famous myth that has been the backbone of many an ugly interaction. It's heard so often and sounds so natural that men and women (and children) often think that it makes intuitive sense. What are the real truths and fallacies in this line of thinking? Was this a theme in your family?

1. When have **you** purposely hurt someone you loved?

2. What did you learn from that experience?

3. What still puzzles you about that period of time?

4. How are you different now than you were then?

5. At this time in your life, how would you handle the situation differently?

23

CHAPTER TWO

REMEMBERING

GETTING THE MESSAGE FROM OTHERS

We are all influenced by a combination of the desires, expectations and needs of our friends, family and society in general. The times we live in, our ethnic heritage, even our age and our size can be the impetus for messages that guide us in our lives. Unfortunately, some of these messages do not bear up over many generations of living and changing. Some are appropriate for the teller, but not the listener. Some have been confused over time. Some cause anxiety, some inspire and some inform.

notes/thoughts/ideas
talk to. . .
ask about. . .

MESSAGES FROM OTHERS CAN LEAVE YOU FEELING HAPPY OR SAD OR ANXIOUS OR FEARFUL, EVEN IF THE MESSAGES WERE SENT WHEN YOU WERE A CHILD AND YOU ARE NOW AN ADULT. RECOGNIZING THE EMOTIONAL IMPACT IS A BEGINNING STEP IN SORTING OUT YOUR PRESENT DAY VALUES.

Since these messages influence us, whether or not we want them to, it is essential to determine where they come from and how much they have formed our sense of what is important. These messages need to be decoded and updated to understand their relevance in our lives. Some we will want to discard, others we will embrace, and yet others we will not fully understand until later in our lives.

When John was a child, his father berated him for not doing better in school and for not being a star athlete. John lacked self-confidence as a young man and had difficulty making friends and taking risks to accomplish things that he wanted in his life. As he grew to adulthood, he went to college, received a degree in business administration, played intramural sports, got married and had a child of his own.

But underneath the "success" in his life as an adult (and no one was prouder of John than his father!) was the gnawing feeling that he wasn't good enough - that he wasn't achieving what he should be, that no one really cared for him. He was suspicious that his wife was interested in other men and that he was about to be passed over for promotions in his work. Even though his life seemed to be running smoothly on the surface, John knew that underneath brewed a mass of anxiety; but he didn't know why.

John was a victim of messages that had been sent to him at an early age. Even though his father "lightened up" in his expectations for John as John grew older ,the weight of his early years and his father's demanding nature remained in his feelings. As an adult it was necessary for him to re-examine those early messages and decide what they had to do with his present life and circumstances: which parts were true, which parts were not - who was he in relation to the messages he had received long ago?

With encouragement from a friend who had looked at similar issues in therapy, John found the courage to speak to his father about his confusion regarding his father's behavior to him when he was a child. One afternoon while sitting in the park, John heard, for the first time, how his father had been belittled by his own parents - how they had punished him for not achieving and led him to believe that he was disgracing the family by not following in their career footsteps. That one afternoon of talking erased years of hurt and bitterness - for the first time he was able to understand why his father had been so cruel. We was also able to feel compassion for his father's sadness in his own life.

" Come back in the house, son, I need to tell you some things about my own family. It's time for us to talk."

Throughout TROUBLE IN PARADISE, you will have the opportunity to reflect on the messages that have been given to you by others. You will be encouraged to view these messages as invaluable tools for understanding your past, present and future. Learn to listen to these internal guides with an ear to understanding the histories and life dilemmas of the people who gave you these guidelines. Try to see their struggles using the same compassion that you will bring to understanding your life and that of your partner. **One thing is certain: the more clearly you can understand the impact of the messages from the world around you, the better chance you will have to relieve anxiety and confusion about your own values and priorities. And the better chance you will have to pass this information on to the partner in your life.**

MESSAGES FROM OTHERS OVER THE YEARS
WHAT DIFFERENCE DID THEY MAKE?

FILL IN THE CHART BELOW AND USE IT AS A STARTING POINT FOR SHARING INFORMATION WITH YOUR PARTNER:

notes/thoughts/ideas
talk to. . .
ask about. . .

Think in terms of "should" messages such as, "You should do this," or "You should be that. . ."

Don't forget messages that were never spoken out loud, but came through loud and clear anyway.

Message	From Whom?	Why Was It Important to the Sender?	How Does This Message Affect <u>You</u> Today?
You should:			
go to college			
dress like a lady(man)			
make $____ a year			
go in the army			
lose weight			
talk more (less)			
change friends			

29

MESSAGES RECEIVED BY YOUR FAMILY AND FRIENDS
WHAT DIFFERENCE DID IT MAKE?

notes/thoughts/ideas
talk to. . .
ask about. . .

Fill out the following chart with information about the messages received by family members and friends.

Who?	Message Received	Sent By Whom?	How Did It Affect His/Her Life?
e.g. Mike	"You're a bum!"	His uncle George	He feels and acts like a bum!
Carly	"You're smart enough to be President!"	Her whole family	She's got great confidence and is very successful.

1. What's the connection between the messages received and how your friends and family live their lives?

2. Who do you know who has worked especially hard to get past negative messages?

3. Who has worked especially hard to live up to positive messages?

4. Can you think of the same message that affects two different people in two different ways? (e.g. one person feels pressured by praise, the other uses it to his or her advantage).

FAMILY TIES THAT BIND

Your roots - your background - is a telling bit of information about who you are today. You may hail from Michigan or England or Hawaii, but no matter where you grew up and called home, you are a product of that personal history. And your history not only includes the geographic locations of your younger years, but also the social and political circumstances that formed your values and your attitudes. Was your family rich or poor? Were family members vocal in community politics? Were they religious? Were they professional people or businessmen and women or were they skilled laborers? Were they college graduates or high school dropouts? Are you?

notes/thoughts/ideas
talk to. . .
ask about. . .

John and Grace lived together for three years. They spent many hours talking about the lives they led before they met and they regaled each other with stories of their personal histories. But when they attended the big family reunion at the wedding of Grace's cousin, they discovered that they had underestimated the significance of much of Grace's family story.

For instance, both John and Grace were surprised (and delighted) to see how much Grace looked and acted like her Great-Aunt Sarah, a woman who had come to the United States on a freighter at the turn of the century. At the wedding, John saw many of the traits that Grace disliked in him, magnified in her father! And, for the first time, they both realized how Grace's ideas about relationships were a direct result of trying to be "different from her parents" - people who had gone through an ugly divorce when she was a teenager.

John and Grace used the time together to observe and reflect on the cross-connections between old and young and different cultures. What could have been a field day for creating distance developed into an adventure in understanding. Instead of being distressed by the problems they saw, they chose to see Grace's history as an exciting key to their future.

Family ties are some of the strongest bonds that you develop as a human being. Even if you don't like everything about your family, chances are you will feel a strong pull to be closer to them, or at least resolve your differences as you get older. Learning how you have moved for or against your own history will give you insights to develop your "new" family's bonding. This information can be a back-up for what you are experiencing now - starting a family that will have strong family ties.

YOUR FAMILY'S STRONGEST TRAITS

Imagine telling a story about what makes your family unique. What is the story?

1. Does this story make you laugh or cry?

2. Do you share the family characteristics illustrated in this story? Are you proud of being similar or dissimilar to your family?

3. What values do you carry with you as a result of your childhood experiences? What motto do you have as an adult that was acquired when you were a child?

4. What are your struggles that came from childhood? What are you trying to leave behind?

5. What surprises you about how you have or haven't changed since you were a child?

ALL THROUGH YOUR LIFE 'FAMILY TIES' WILL BECKON TO YOU AND INSIST THAT YOU PAY ATTENTION. YOU MAY TRAVEL FAR DOWN THE ROAD TOWARD BEING COMFORTABLE WITH YOUR OWN VALUE SYSTEM, GOALS AND EXPECTATIONS, BUT YOUR 'FAMILY TIES' WILL STILL ECHO IN THE DISTANCE.

YOUR PARTNER WILL COME TO THE RELATIONSHIP WITH HIS OR HER OWN SET OF TIES THAT MIGHT BE REASSURING OR CONSTRAINING. IT IS IMPORTANT TO WORK TOGETHER TO ESTABLISH COMMON GROUND IN THIS NEW FAMILY YOU ARE CREATING TOGETHER. YOUR VISION WILL BE UNIQUE TO YOU AS NEW PARTNERS YET IT WILL ALWAYS BE SHAPED BY THE FAMILY EXPERIENCES THAT HAVE GONE BEFORE.

FAMILY EXPECTATIONS AND ROLE MODELS

DRAW A PICTURE OF YOU BEING HELD TO YOUR FAMILY BY STRINGS.

notes/thoughts/ideas
talk to. . .
ask about. . .

What do these strings represent (money? guilt? family loyalty? secrets?) Give them labels.

THINK ABOUT THESE QUESTIONS:

1. When did these strings first develop?

2. When you were younger, did they feel positive or negative? What about now that you are an adult?

3. What does your partner notice and say about your strings to your family?

4. What can you tell him/her to help create a better understanding of how you are connected to your family history?

5. In what ways are your partner's family ties similar to your own? Does this create a climate for understanding or <u>mis</u>understanding each other?

SHARE YOUR THOUGHTS WITH YOUR PARTNER

33

UNDERSTANDING YOUR PARTNER'S FAMILY HISTORY

notes/thoughts/ideas
talk to. . .
ask about. . .

What do you think is the most important aspect of your partner's personal history?

What have you learned from your partner's family history that gives you clues about things you might want to do in your own life?

COMPLETE THE FOLLOWING SENTENCES:

When I think about his/her family, I'm concerned about _____

_____

When it comes to my partner's family, I really like _____

_____

One thing I don't understand about his/her family is why _____

_____

When it comes to his/her family, I hope _____

_____

His/her family history is different than mine in that _____

_____

SHARE YOUR RESPONSES WITH YOUR PARTNER

I'VE HAD THIS PROBLEM BEFORE!

If a conflict situation isn't really understood or resolved, but is merely set aside while you go on with your life, there is a good chance it will come back to haunt you over and over again. Sometimes an old conflict will take another form, but if you reflect on the feelings that you have in a current situation, you can often recognize the same dynamics at work.

notes/thoughts/ideas
talk to...
ask about...

John and Claire generally got along well. They had understandings about housework and auto maintenance and who would take care of the children on the weekends. But when it came to evenings spent with friends, they could never agree. John wanted to go out after work with his friends from college and spend time playing cards and drinking beer. Claire liked to stay at home with the kids and wanted John there, too. She became incensed whenever this issue came up. She accused John of not caring about her and the children and their time together.

Everytime they fought over time spent with friends instead of with the family, Claire had a nagging feeling that she was running through some pretty old scenes in her life, but she couldn't understand why it bothered her as much as it did. Spending an afternoon alone, she took out a pen and paper and began to write - tracing her feelings backwards from relationship to relationship - trying to find clues as to why John's socializing caused her to be so angry and feel so rejected.

Reviewing her description of her string of boyfriends over the years, she came to realize that from the first date with her first "boyfriend" in high school she had been very threatened by the men in her life having other close friends. In high school she had managed to keep her boyfriend from seeing other people, but in later and more mature relationships, men tended to see her as being too possessive and demanding and the relationship would end.

Writing about these painful memories allowed Claire to look one step further. She eventually realized that her feelings were connected with her mother's fears about her father's absences, and the turmoil it had caused in the household when she was younger. Claire's father would be away with his friends for days and nights on end. He wasn't home for birthdays or graduations or soccer games. Her mother was often frantic with worry and anger. The issue of outside friends became a battleground that distressed the whole family for years.

notes/thoughts/ideas
talk to. . .
ask about. . .

Problem areas that are not resolved can become more than "problems" for us. They can evolve into real life dramas of despair and depression. This is especially true if they involve our loved ones, for those are the situations that require more attention than to our own needs and desires.

Sometimes men and women feel guilty over the recurrence of a particularly negative theme in their lives. They may berate themselves for not having a handle on the problem, for not moving on. But patterns in life are the rule not the exception. Though we may have great intentions for learning and growing, we tend to behave as we have in the past. It takes steady attention to the dynamics of our inner lives to make headway against old patterns.

There is much to learn about how we approach solutions and fall back into old ways of being. The more we learn, the faster we can move toward permanent change in areas that are important to us, and help our partners do the same.

"Why do you keep going over this same issue every single time we have an argument? Are you ever going to let it go?"

PRACTICE LOOKING AT "RECURRING THEMES" IN YOUR LIFE, NOT WITH AN AIR OF DEFENSIVENESS OR GUILT, BUT WITH INTEREST AND COMPASSION FOR HUMAN CHALLENGES. TAKE THIS OPPORTUNITY TO ACCEPT WHAT HAVE BEEN NEGATIVE PATTERNS AND RECOGNIZE THAT IT MAY WELL BE TIME TO TAKE THE FIRST STEPS TOWARD FINDING SOLUTIONS FOR BEHAVIORS AND RESPONSES THAT HAVE NOT SERVED YOU WELL IN THE PAST.

On the following pages, you will have the chance to look at specific conflicts that you have encountered in your life. The exercises allow you to reflect on when they first appeared, how you arrived at solutions, who and what you used as resources, and what feelings walked hand-in-hand with these dilemmas.

PERSONAL CONFLICTS THAT ARE A THEME IN MY LIFE

What is a conflict in your personal life that has appeared over and over again?

notes/thoughts/ideas
talk to. . .
ask about. . .

**LABEL THE TIME LINE BELOW SHOWING WHEN, OVER THE YEARS, THIS PROBLEM
WAS PRESENT:**

first time I
remember it

the last time it
happened

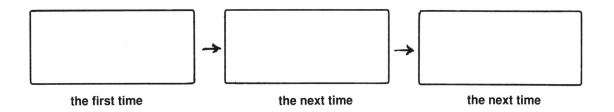

the first time   the next time   the next time

**In each of the boxes above, write key words to describe the circumstances and the
feelings that you associate with the conflict.**

**How do you feel <u>now</u> when you think and talk about this recurring theme in your
personal life?**

37

CAREER CONFLICTS THAT ARE A THEME IN MY LIFE

What is a conflict in your career that has appeared over and over again?

**LABEL THE TIME LINE BELOW SHOWING WHEN, OVER THE YEARS, THIS PROBLEM
WAS PRESENT:**

first time I   the last time
remember it   it happened

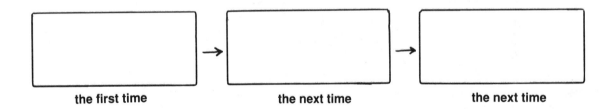

the first time   the next time   the next time

**In each of the boxes above, write key words to describe the circumstances and the
feelings that you associate with the conflict.**

**How do you feel <u>now</u> when you think and talk about this recurring theme in your
career?**

38

RELATIONSHIP CONFLICTS THAT ARE A THEME IN MY LIFE

What is a relationship conflict that has appeared over and over in your life?

**LABEL THE TIME LINE BELOW SHOWING WHEN, OVER THE YEARS, THIS PROBLEM
WAS PRESENT:**

first time I
remember it

the last time
it happened

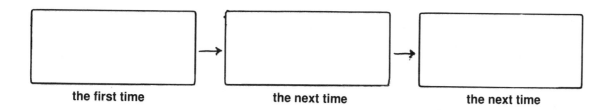

the first time   the next time   the next time

In each of the boxes above, write key words to describe the circumstances and the
feelings that you associate with this relationship conflict.

How do you feel <u>now</u> when you think and talk about this recurring theme in your
relationships?

39

WHY DID WE GET TOGETHER IN THE FIRST PLACE?

Remember why you got together in the first place? Now that time has passed you may look with favor or with horror upon the motivations and assumptions that brought you together as a couple.

notes/thoughts/ideas
talk to. . .
ask about. . .

When Janice and Kim met, it was a "rebound" story. They had both broken up with long-term partners in the months past and were reeling from the experience of being alone and feeling lonely. Janice and Kim both had definite ideas about the kind of relationship they wanted, and they were sure that their new ideals had nothing to do with what had happened in the past.

Janice's previous boyfriend had been physically violent and extremely jealous. The three years they lived together were filled with brutal arguments. Kim and his previous girlfriend had a lukewarm relationship. They got along well but had "no sparks", and after a series of increasingly bitter debates, they parted ways.

Janice and Kim were a match made in heaven, or so it seemed. Kim gravitated toward the feisty personality of Janice and she loved the calm demeanor that Kim brought to their time together. Neither of them could believe how different it was to be in this "new" partnership. They appreciated the things in each other that their previous partners had despised. But as time went on Janice and Kim got over the effects of being newly-separated and then newly-attached and the more basic aspects of their feelings and histories started to surface. And they didn't always like what they were seeing.

Janice's gutsy independence began to bother Kim. Kim's quiet, steadfast attitudes began to bore Janice. They lost the "glow" of infatuation and began to seriously question what their relationship was about.

If you find yourself at this stage of the game, it's time to re-remember the initial momentum and life circumstances that were present when you decided you would like to be a couple and would like to be parents. Maybe you weren't completely "tuned in" to all of the intricacies and subtleties that might arise later on when "the glow" wore off, but this in no way means that you must discard the relationship you now have because it is different from the one you thought you were taking on.

Does this sound complex? It isn't. We begin all life situations with one set of expectations and assumptions, but we are constantly revising our opinions and goals and perceptions as we see more of the picture and as we seek to fit that picture into our lives or ourselves into it. If we move on, discarding the old as soon as it loses its gloss, we will never be able to learn to enjoy the intimacy and depth that only comes with time and shared history.

Indeed, what can we expect to know of a friend and lover in the first days, months or even years? Is it realistic to expect, in that period of time, to have more than a shadow view of this person that we may well be choosing as a lifetime mate? Yet many of us take this stance: we assume that the person to whom we have emotionally attached ourselves has revealed the most important parts of his or her life to us, and there won't be many surprises later on. Surely we hope there won't be surprises that will catch us off guard, or cause us to rethink or review our vows and commitments.

If the first step is re-remembering why you got together in the first place, the second step is re-evaluating. What is different now? How are you different? How are your personal goals different? How are you the same? What about your partner? How is she or he the same? How has she or he changed? How for the better? How for the worse? Why?

When Janice and Kim did the following exercise, they were stuck in thinking it was unfair that their feelings had changed, that their partner wasn't the person they thought he or she was in the beginning, that life was different now and their relationship didn't fit with the new set of life circumstances. But underneath, their initial attraction to each other kept them struggling to reaffirm their desire to be together. This was the "catch" that Janice and Kim learned to honor. They could admit that many parts were different, that they had learned about each other and found some things they <u>didn't</u> like (but some they did!).

*"The first time I saw you, I loved the way
you laughed with your brothers and sisters."*

They could see that not everything lived up to their expectations, but they could make those new expectations just as exciting, and more realistic, with some concentrated examination of what had happened to them both along the way.

WHAT BROUGHT YOU TOGETHER IN THE FIRST PLACE?

1. What did you like and dislike about how your partner looked? About his or her personality?

2. What did your partner bring out in <u>you</u> that you liked?

3. What did you like or dislike about your partner's family?

4. What did you think would be different with him or her than with your previous partners? Why did you think this?

5. What did he or she do that made you especially happy?

6. How did you describe this new relationship to your friends and family?

DO YOURSELF AND YOUR PARTNER A FAVOR BY SPENDING SOME TIME EACH DAY REMEMBERING WHAT IT WAS THAT MADE YOU THINK (AND MORE IMPORTANTLY, MADE YOU <u>FEEL</u>) THAT YOU COULD BE INTIMATE PARTNERS AND SHARE PARENTING WITH EASE AND LOVE.

43

<u>NOW</u>, WHAT DO YOU THINK BROUGHT YOU TOGETHER?

notes/thoughts/ideas
talk to. . .
ask about. . .

FINISH THE FOLLOWING SENTENCES:

1. As much as I hate to admit it, I thought _____

2. It makes me feel silly now, but I believed that _____

3. Now I can see that when I met him (or her) I needed to _____

4. One of the things that I was attracted to is _____

5. My family influenced me to love him (or her) by saying _____

6. My friends influenced me to love him (or her) by saying _____

7. When I met him (or her) I was running away from _____

8. I had never met anyone before who _____

9. For the first time in my life, I was able to _____

10. In this relationship, I thought that I would get _____

SHARE YOUR THOUGHTS AND REFLECTIONS WITH YOUR PARTNER

**USE THE FOLLOWING CHARTS TO EXAMINE "CHANGE" IN YOUR LIFE.
WHAT DO YOU THINK AND FEEL ABOUT THESE CHANGES?**

THIS IS HOW I HAVE CHANGED SINCE WE FIRST MET:

notes/thoughts/ideas
talk to. . .
ask about. . .

This was before:	This is now:	This is how I feel:	This is what I think:

REFLECT ON THESE QUESTIONS AND SHARE YOUR THOUGHTS WITH YOUR PARTNER:

1. What changes do you feel good about? bad about? why?

2. Which changes are a result of having achieved some of your goals?

3. Which changes has your partner been an integral part of?

THIS IS HOW <u>MY PARTNER</u> HAS CHANGED

notes/thoughts/ideas talk to. . . ask about. . .	This was before:	This is now:	This is how I feel:	This is what I think:

REFLECT ON THESE QUESTIONS WITH YOUR PARTNER:

1. What are his or her feelings and thoughts about <u>your</u> perceptions of the changes you have both gone through?

2. Which changes caused one partner to feel good and the other to feel bad?

3. Which are a result of new goals and goals attained?

4. Which changes caused you both to feel satisfied? puzzled? sad? frightened? disappointed? elated? Why?

46

THIS IS HOW <u>OUR RELATIONSHIP</u> HAS CHANGED

This was before:	This is now:	This is how I feel:	This is what I think:

notes/thoughts/ideas
talk to. . .
ask about. . .

REFLECT ON THESE QUESTIONS WITH YOUR PARTNER:

1. Which of these changes causes you to feel sad? disappointed? glad? relieved? Why?

2. Which of these changes did you expect?

3. In retrospect, which of these changes <u>should</u> you have expected?

4. Which of these changes did someone tell you to expect?

AND NOW WHAT?

FINISH THE FOLLOWING SENTENCES AND SHARE YOUR RESPONSES WITH YOUR PARTNER:

Since we first got together,

I'm glad _____

I appreciate _____

I've been happy with _____

You've helped me by _____

I've tried to make you happy by _____

I've learned to _____

I've become more aware of _____

I'm grateful for _____

I've enjoyed _____

I'm looking forward to _____

THINK ABOUT THESE QUESTIONS:
1. How did you feel when you finished the above sentences?

2. Was it difficult to say positive things about your partnership? Why?

3. Can you think of more affirmations that weren't listed above? What are they?

MYTH NUMBER TWO
EVERYONE IN MY FAMILY GETS DIVORCED;
I'M JUST LIKE THEM

The models our families give us for our expectations and behaviors cannot be dismissed lightly. If we see that our parents or other family members have had a difficult time achieving rewarding partnerships, we may well have fears about succeeding ourselves. If we haven't had a model for how people work out differences, we may have no idea where to begin.

notes/thoughts/ideas
talk to. . .
ask about. . .

1. Who in your family has a "good" relationship ? What have you learned from them? How are you like them? How are you different?

2. Which couple in your family would you not like to emulate? What have you learned from them? How are you like them? How are you different? If they could give you a lesson on having rewarding relationships, what would they say?

3. Are you afraid that your family will resent you if you succeed where they have failed?

4. No matter what the "success or failure rate" of the other couples in your family, there is much to learn if you observe closely. Will it be easier for you to follow the family pattern of divorce?

CHAPTER THREE

TIMING

HEY, HOW LONG IS THIS GOING TO TAKE?

It's not unusual for friends and family to get "worn out" waiting for someone to make it through a major life transition. This life passage might be adolescence, career change, a move to a new town, or recovery after a long illness. It might also be divorce or having a baby. As we work through our life passages, we are operating according to our own internal sense of "how long it should take" to reach the end of the stage. Sometimes the exasperation of loved ones will force us to take the leap to the next level. At times a message may come from an unexpected source that tells us it's time to make decisions, change behavior, work toward new perceptions - "move on."

notes/thoughts/ideas
talk to. . .
ask about. . .

Don and Corey were experiencing a sense of "Hey, wait a minute. Isn't this getting adjusted to being new parents going on way too long?" They expected the adjustments to level out after the first few weeks: the baby would be sleeping through the night, they would be making love (again!) on a regular basis, Corey would lose weight quickly and be back in good physical shape, they would feel like traveling with the baby, and things would generally be light and airy in their lives.

Big surprise! After five months, little Hans still didn't sleep through the night. Friends told them everything from 'You should check with a child psychologist" to "No problem, it might be a year before he does" to "How come you can't get him on a better schedule?" After five months, Corey still didn't feel like making love; she had sore breasts from nursing, she felt bombarded with attention from the baby and Don, and she was always tired. Friends' advice ranged from "See a counselor" to "Get a divorce" to "No problem, it takes at least two years!" You can guess the stories and advice that went along with the other expectations.

"Well, how long did we think it was going to take? After all, we did just have a baby!"

53

Don and Corey may have been a couple struggling with the not-too-surprising elements of new parenthood. They may have been in the process of coming up with solutions to problems and attitudes that come quite naturally with a major life change in circumstances. On the other hand, they may also have been in the throes of another natural life phenomenon - Postpartum Depression and its effects on the new mother and father.

THE FACTS ABOUT POSTPARTUM ADJUSTMENT

For the many, many people who experience mild or severe depression (and possibly a real emotional break with reality) after the birth of a child, making the adjustments that have to do with being a parent is just not that easy, and may seem impossible, at least for a period of time. Problems that were dealt with before the birth may seem quite insurmountable afterwards and this reduction in the ability to "deal with" what is going on is no fluke. It has a very real base in the physiology of women during the pregnancy and birth experience and may have only tangentially to do with a couple's ability or motivation to "work out" problems.

Here is the news about Postpartum Depression and what new parents should be aware of as a possibility in understanding their own life circumstances before and after having a child. Postpartum Depression strikes a majority of women - some statistics say that 80% of women are affected. It occurs because of the natural drop in hormone levels after the birth of a baby. Pre-birth hormone levels are running at a level that may be fifty times higher than that of the pre-pregnancy state. Immediately after the delivery, when the placenta leaves the body, the progesterone hormone level drops dramatically, and many women feel a sense of depression and anxiety associated with this. This stage usually sets in about three days after the birth - unfortunately, this is also the time when women who have given birth in the hospital are heading home to start their new life as parents.

For years, it was thought that the stresses of taking the baby home, having the added responsibilities and adjustments to the new couple/parent relationship were the cause of these "baby blues." So as women struggled to rise above the "baby blues," and new fathers did everything they could to be understanding and helpful, they often felt inadequate to the task - even wondering whether or not they really wanted to have this child and be in the relationship that had created the space for having a baby. These are frightening thoughts for a new father and a new mother. In general, this sense of unease provides the base for an even greater anxiety, because the feelings run counter to the expectation that motherhood will bring on a burst of bonding and warmth and ease at fulfilling a "woman's role" in society.

So, the three day mark can be crucial in a physiological sense for the new mother, as it triggers psychological symptoms that may be quite disturbing. Now, if that was the only transition, and it only took a few days, it might be a small enough (though none-the-less-upsetting) period of time that both parents could hang in there until it was over. Unfortunately, although once again quite naturally,

54

many women then experience a new set of symptoms and changes at the three week mark. At this point, the body experiences a decrease in thyroid hormone- a condition that is accompanied by listlessness, depression and lack of sexual energy. Even for those who are not recovering from the challenges of birthing, low thyroid in the system brings with it these same physiological and psychological symptoms.

Understanding these delicate time frames that attend almost every birthing experience to a greater or lesser degree, can provide moral support that new parents need. We would hope that every parent would be informed about these natural stages of transition, but the sad case is that millions of men and women know nothing about this process that occurs in the body, know nothing about the commonality of the stress that accompanies these bodily changes, and are left feeling desperate for a context in which to understand the thoughts and feelings that are running rampant in the new family. Although the extent of postpartum adjustment and depression has been documented for centuries, it is only in very recent years that there has been much attention given to the dissemination of this information to the general public. Physicians, psychiatrists and other professionals who work in the helping professions may have as little information about this physiological phenomenon and its effects on the new parents as do the new parents themselves. But that picture is changing and will change more rapidly in the coming years as Postpartum Depression support groups spring up across the country and medical professionals become more informed about this field and the variety of treatments that can ease the symptoms until the physiological transition period is over.

IT IS IMPORTANT TO REALIZE THAT EVEN AFTER THE HORMONAL LEVELS RETURN TO "NORMAL" IN THE WOMAN'S BODY, THE SENSE OF VULNERABILITY AND ANXIETY THAT MAY HAVE OCCURRED DURING THE TRANSITION CAN STILL LEAVE THEIR MARK ON THE PERSONALITY AND ATTITUDES OF THE NEW MOTHER, AS WELL AS THE NEW FATHER AND THEIR COUPLE RELATIONSHIP.

FOR THIS REASON, IT IS EXTREMELY IMPORTANT FOR NEW PARENTS TO BE KNOWLEDGEABLE ABOUT THIS NATURAL PROCESS, OFFER ACTIVE SUPPORT AND UNDERSTANDING TO EACH OTHER, AND PASS ON THE INFORMATION ABOUT THIS CRUCIAL PERIOD OF TIME TO OTHER NEW PARENTS WHO MAY BE EXPERIENCING SIMILAR TIMES OF DISTRESS WITHOUT UNDERSTANDING WHY.

55

PREGNANCY AND TRANSITION

What were your "time for transition" expectations with respect to pregnancy and childbirth?

FILL OUT THE FOLLOWING CHART.

Write in the amount of time that you thought it would take to be back to "normal" and the time it actually took.

Some or all of the items may speak to your concerns. Answer the ones that do, and add your own.

	How long did you <u>think</u> it would take?	How long <u>did</u> it take?
To regain "normal" sexual relations with your partner		
To regain body tone, weight		
To regain sense of energy & vitality		
To be ready to go back to work		
To:		
To:		
To:		
To:		
To:		

Postpartum Depression is just one of the areas where couples and parents must imagine the possibility of having to adjust their sense of "How long is this going to take?" when they are looking at transitions between life stages. Because all individuals move at their own pace, you can have conflict when your time table runs counter to others. It is essential to understand how your partner sees the passage of time and how he or she evaluates the "time needed" to traverse life passages. It is also valuable to know how your partner likes to be treated when he or she is struggling with a life dilemma. Just as there are differences in timing, so there are a variety of ways that people prefer to be treated during a time of crisis.

WHEN YOU ARE IN THE MIDDLE OF A CRISIS OR COMPLEX LIFE CHANGE, HOW DO <u>YOU</u> PREFER THAT OTHERS HELP YOU?

I prefer:

_____ to be left alone
_____ to be coaxed to talk
_____ to be coddled
_____ that others do not acknowledge my situation
_____ that others do acknowledge my situation
_____ to get suggestions from others
_____ to get no suggestions from anyone
_____ to give the cues about what they should do

WHEN SOMEONE CLOSE TO YOU IS IN THE MIDDLE OF A CRISIS OR COMPLEX LIFE CHANGE, HOW DO YOU LIKE TO BE PART OF HELPING OUT?

_____ I don't like to be part of helping out
_____ I like to ask questions
_____ I like to acknowledge that I see what is going on
_____ I like to offer suggestions
_____ I like to be off to the side, but accessible if the person wants my advice
_____ I like to suggest books to read and things to do that might help

SHARE THESE THOUGHTS AND FEELINGS WITH YOUR PARTNER

GETTING BACK TO "NORMAL"

FILL OUT THE CHART BELOW.

Indicate how long you would "realistically" expect it to take for an individual to regain equilibrium (be back to "normal") after going through the events listed. What would your partner say?

EVENT	YOUR TIME FRAME	YOUR PARTNER'S TIME FRAME
A major career change		
An automobile accident		
The death of a parent		
A move from an established home		
The birth of a child		
Major surgery		
Divorce		
Changing a bad habit		

Think of the people you have known who have had these experiences.

1. What was their "recovery" time? <u>Did</u> they recover?

2. Have you ever thought that someone got over a major change too quickly? Why?

3. Have you ever thought that someone took way too long to make an adjustment?
   Why did you think this?

From filling out the chart on the previous page, what areas in your life can you imagine might be conflict spots for you and your partner because of differences in perception about the time it takes to "get back to normal"?

notes/thoughts/ideas
talk to. . .
ask about. . .

1.

2.

3.

What conflicts have you already experienced that have to do with this issue?

For what issues do you have very similar ideas or time frames?

Remember a situation in your life that required you to adapt to <u>someone else's</u> transition time. What was it?

Did you feel happy with the degree of support you were able to give?

Did the other person agree with the value of your efforts?

What did you learn from that experience?

How are you different <u>now</u> as a result of that experience?

59

Remember a situation that required someone else to adapt to <u>your</u> life transition. What was the transition?

Did you feel satisfied with the degree of support they were able to give you?

Did they feel comfortable with their ability to be supportive?

What did you learn from that experience?

How are you different <u>now</u> as a result of that experience?

WHEN YOUR TIME LINES SAY IT'S TIME TO BE THROUGH WITH A DIFFICULT TRANSITION, YET THE EMOTIONAL DETAILS STILL HAVEN'T BEEN THOROUGHLY UNDERSTOOD OR WORKED OUT, THE RESULT CAN BE CONFUSION, FRUSTRATION AND EVEN DESPAIR. IT'S IMPORTANT TO GET A CLEAR SENSE OF JUST HOW YOU AND YOUR PARTNER MOVE THROUGH TIMES OF STRESS AND LIFE CHANGE. ONLY WITH THIS INFORMATION CAN YOU OPEN THE DOOR TO BEING SUPPORTIVE, RATHER THAN EXASPERATED PARTNERS.

FIRST THINGS FIRST

Sometimes your behavior can tell you more about what is important to you than your words. When you find yourself in a situation where what is happening isn't even close to what you <u>say</u> you would <u>like</u> to be happening, you can choose to listen to your words or to watch your actions. If the actions don't match the words, it is probably time to examine "priorities."

Your priorities are what you deem to be of importance to you. Without seriously considering the value you place on the activities of your daily life, you may feel that you are drifting from event to event without rhyme or reason. The result is a juggling act that carries a load of anxiety and double messages.

Night after night Leon called from the office to tell Betsy that he'd be home within the hour. Night after night Betsy waited for Leon to arrive, but he would not show up until several hours later. When Betsy repeatedly exploded with anger at this behavior, which she labeled " gross inconsideration," Leon was shocked and angry in return. Couldn't she see that he was working those hours to support the family? Wasn't it obvious that he was too busy to call her and change the time that he would be arriving? How could she think that his being late meant anything at all in terms of his caring for her?

These questions and recriminations kept Betsy and Leon going around in circles for years. Her friends thought she was a fool to put up with it. His friends thought she was a nagging wife who didn't appreciate his efforts. She waited for him. He was late. She got very angry. He got even angrier. She felt guilty for wanting his time. He felt guilty for not giving it.

Betsy and Leon were caught by unclear priorities. Betsy knew that Leon cared for her, but she felt that he was saying a great deal more by staying at

"If you love me, why do you break your agreements with me? Show me you care by following through on what you say."

61

the office and putting substantially more time into his work than into their relationship. It wasn't enough for her to know that he was earning money for the family. She would have preferred to have less money and more time together as a couple and as a family. Leon felt that his intentions were obvious. He loved Betsy and wanted to be in a partnership with her. But he was also drawn to his work and to providing financial security for the family, and his work was requiring an immense amount of time for him to be successful.

Betsy and Leon sat down one night after dinner and wrote out their priorities. They examined what was important to each of them, why it was important, and what commitments they could make to see "top priority" items have "top priority time" allotted to them.

On the following pages you will be able to examine the priorities that you have established in your life and talk about these priorities with your partner. If you haven't spent much time in the past considering these issues, you may find it difficult to categorize and explain your thoughts and feelings. Use the information you come up with to make headway in this very serious area of partner communication. You will find that this exercise not only helps your partner understand your directions, but will also enlighten you as to your own goals and daily plans.

DON'T BE SURPRISED IF YOU FIND THAT YOU HAVE GIVEN "LIP SERVICE" TO SOME AREAS OF YOUR LIFE - THAT YOUR ACTUAL BEHAVIOR <u>HASN'T</u> MATCHED YOUR INTENTIONS. THESE MAY BE THE ISSUES THAT HAVE "DRIVEN YOUR PARTNER CRAZY," BUT THEY HAVE ALSO TAKEN THEIR TOLL ON <u>YOUR</u> ABILITY TO PROCEED WITH YOUR <u>OWN</u> CHOSEN LIFE GOALS.

PRIORITIES

**FILL OUT THE CHART BELOW, PLACING ISSUES AND TASKS IN THE
APPROPRIATE QUADRANTS** (i.e. doing errands, going to the office, driving
the kids around, playing sports).

Think in terms of relationship and personal issues.

Put stars next to those that have to do with "being a couple"

**A - Very important tasks and issues
Must be dealt with immediately**

**B - Very important tasks and
issues; Do not have to be
dealt with immediately**

**C - Tasks and issues that are
not very important;
But must be dealt with
immediately**

**D - Tasks and issues that are
not very important; Do
not have to be dealt with
immediately**

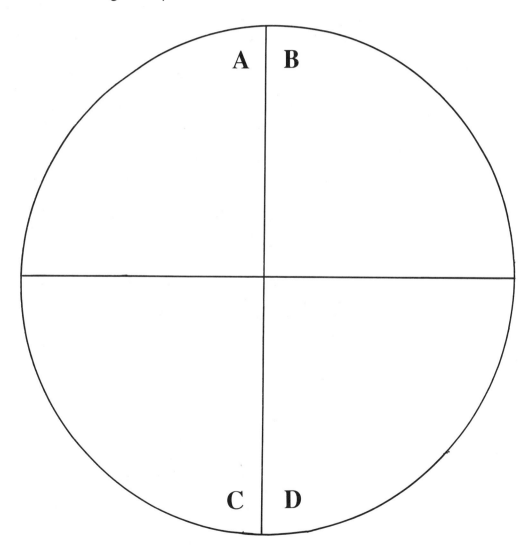

TAKE A LOOK AT THESE FOUR CATEGORIES OF PRIORITIES

A - TASKS AND ISSUES (Very important; must be dealt with immediately)

Rating: TOP PRIORITY

This means that they are of great importance/mean a lot to you (or someone else) and need to be dealt with right away.

Description: Are often deeply felt, long-standing issues that have not been previously addressed by one or both partners. They may not even have to do with the partners themselves, but be hold overs from other parts of your life. Nevertheless, you can't just will them to go away, and if you try, they will resurface later or attach to a different situation, muddying those waters, too.

What will happen if you disregard these tasks and issues?:

They <u>must</u> be addressed to keep your relationship at a minimal level of acceptability - if not, yo will build hostility and distance from your partner.

Questions to consider:

1. Is it possible that you are actually seeking to create distance from your partner? Why?

2. If this issue is not resolved, will you be extremely anxious, bitter or angry?

3. If you fail to come to agreement, what are the possible consequences for your relationship? These consequences may appear as feelings or actions.

REMEMBER THAT ADDRESSING AN ISSUE IN A MANNER THAT DEMONSTRATES THOUGHTFULNESS AND CARING FOR MUTUAL CONCERNS IS A MAJOR FIRST STEP. RESOLUTION DOES NOT NECESSARILY MEAN COMING TO AN AGREEMENT.

Do you have a lot of items in the "A" category ?

If so, it may mean that:

1. You haven't been communicating your concerns as they come up, stockpiling them until they become a huge package. Remember that Type A items will have their day, and not necessarily when you want them to. So keep your slate clean and update your issues with your partner.
2. You have many heartfelt issues that may be difficult to sort out without the help of a professional counselor or therapist.
3. Your partner has not been acknowledging your concerns and they have been building up over time.

Why would someone who loves you refuse to acknowledge your concerns?
1. They might have the viewpoint that your life problems are too overwhelming. They may be keeping a safe distance to maintain their own equilibrium.
2. They may not know what to say or how to say what they feel.
3. They may feel responsible for coming up with a solution, and not have any idea what that solution should be.
4. They may not see your perceptions as valid or worthy of attention.
5. The issues may be "too close to home" - they may, in reality, be shared concerns.
6. The issues may be triggering unpleasant associations with parents' quarrels or trouble with past relationships.

ANY OR ALL OF THESE REASONS COULD CAUSE A PARTNER TO "REFUSE TO BE AVAILABLE" TO LOOK AT THE ISSUES THAT ARE MOST VITAL AND PRESSING TO YOU. WHILE YOU SEARCH OUT YOUR OWN PRIORITY ITEMS, YOU MUST ALSO UNDERSTAND THE RESPONSE THAT YOUR PARTNER MAY BE HAVING.

B - TASKS AND ISSUES (Very important; but do not have to be dealt with immediately)

Rating: HIGH PRIORITY

Description: These tasks or issues are the ones most frequently ignored or left out. You can see tha they are important, but since they aren't leaping out and demanding attention, they are continually put aside.

What will happen if you disregard these tasks and issues?
B issues that you ignore long enough will evolve into the more urgent A issues. Many problems in couple relationships fit into this scenario. Couples will wait for months or years before they get up the nerve to talk to their partner about something that has been bothering them ever day. By the time it does come to the forefront, one or the other of the partners has developed a shell that is virtually impenetrable by the other. They have waited too long, and the preventive steps that could have been taken early on are now emergency measures. And, as we know, emergency measures don't always happen soon enough to save the patient.

Another possible scenario is that if you don't pay attention to the "B" tasks that your partner is reporting to you, he or she will find someone else who does value the urgency, and that person will step in to fill the gap. At that point, you may or may not be left behind.

65

Questions to consider:

1. Are you secretly hoping that your partner will find someone else to listen? By not addressing these concerns, are you making the statement that you want your partner to move on to another relationship?

IN A SOCIETY WHERE PEOPLE ARE OFTEN RUNNING "FULL-STEAM AHEAD," BOTH MEN AND WOMEN CAN EASILY TAKE ON THE ROLE OF "CRISIS MANAGER" AND PAY ATTENTION ONLY TO THOSE ITEMS THAT HAVE REACHED THE CRISIS STAGE. THIS BECOMES AN UNENDING CYCLE AND IS A SOURCE OF GREAT ANXIETY. THE BEST WAY TO AVOID THIS CRISIS CYCLE IS TO ADDRESS "B" ITEMS ON A REGULAR BASIS, BEFORE THEY WORK THEIR WAY INTO THE VOLATILE "A" CATEGORY.

C- TASKS AND ISSUES (Not very important, but must be dealt with immediately)

Rating: LOW PRIORITY

Description: "C" issues make up the major part of our lives. They're often the routine tasks that we do every day. But, these tasks are not necessarily important just because they have to be done on a regular basis or right away.

What will happen if you disregard these tasks and issues?:

These are tasks that give our lives a semblance of order and continuity, but if they are disregarded, often someone else will complete them, or the effect on the rest of our lives will be minimal if they aren't completed at all.

Questions to consider:

1. Do your everyday tasks and issues fit in with your long-term life goals and dreams? If not, is it because you are plodding away at the mundane tasks so that you can divert yourself from addressing the "real work" of your life?

2. Do your everyday tasks form a shield against taking new risks? If so, is this because they remind you of accomplishments in the past? What is happening in your present life that requires new behaviors and attention to new tasks instead of old?

3. Do your friends or family ever suggest that you are "spinning your wheels" with activity that isn't related to the bigger picture of your life? Why do they say this? What are they talking about?

D- TASKS AND ISSUES (Not very important, do not have to be dealt with immediately)

Rating: LOWEST PRIORITY

Description: These tasks do not contribute much to the home or the relationship. In fact, they do no contribute much to the person who thinks or worries about them, either.

What happens if you disregard these tasks and issues?

Few people will ever notice if these tasks or issues are ever addressed.

If you disregard "D" tasks it won't hurt you, there will be no (or few) repercussions in terms of your job or your life and no one will be very upset or insist that you do them.

Questions to consider:

1. So why do people ever do these tasks? You may find yourself working on D tasks because they they are easy and you can feel a sense of accomplishment when they're done. The task may be interesting, or you may not have the confidence or skills to do what is really important, what will really make a difference.

(e.g., Pat was the manager of a large business. His duties had to do with keeping a multi-million dollar enterprise together. But Pat wasted huge amounts of time attending to details that secretaries, file clerks and receptionists had been hired to do. He spent hours opening mail and answering routine letters with laborious responses when a quick response would have been sufficient. His co-workers shook their head in amazement, and eventually Pat was moved to a lesser part of the operation. He could never get himself to attack the major managerial parts of the business and actually use the skills that had originally made him an attractive job candidate .

The world is filled with cartoons showing "mom" at home washing windows, cleaning the corners with a toothbrush, and getting the laundry just the right shade of white while life goes on outside . Only she knows if these are personal goals that create immense satisfaction or activities that provide relief while personal goals are kept at bay.

ONLY YOU KNOW WHICH IS TRUE FOR YOU.

CLARIFYING YOUR GOALS AND
FINDING SOLUTIONS TO "TIME BOGS"

notes/thoughts/ideas
talk to. . .
ask about. . .

The problem_____
(i.e. We need to have at least one afternoon a week to go out together and play
sports like we did before we had the baby.)

How I See It   **How He/She Sees It**   **Shared Solutions**
_____

WHERE DOES THE TIME GO?

New parents are rarely prepared for the time commitment that having a baby brings to their lives. They know, of course, that a whole new set of activities will be on line. What they don't fully grasp (and how can they without prior experience?) is the <u>extent</u> of the time that is involved in doing all of these child maintenance tasks, and how, of necessity, it is time that must be carved away from other parts of their lives.

notes/thoughts/ideas
talk to. . .
ask about. . .

Elaine felt she had the "information" she needed before having a baby. She knew that babies need to be fed, changed, held, taken to the doctor when ill, etc. She was certainly prepared for her life to be different from how it was before she had a child (she had worked as a librarian for the six years previous to becoming pregnant). These things all seemed rather obvious to Elaine. What was not obvious, and what Elaine was unprepared for, was the amount of time it was actually going to take to do all of these chores.

Taken one by one the tasks of baby care didn't require much time, but combined they added up to whole days, weeks and months. Elaine and her husband, Bill, found that it could take ten minutes to change a diaper that might well have to be changed again fifteen minutes later. Feeding could take a half hour or two hours, doctor's visits consumed entire days.

"Hey, that was easy! It only took three hours to get out the door.
Too bad we have to be home in twenty minutes!"

When Elaine and Bill wanted to go out together, they grappled with the fact that getting the baby into warm clothing, (after waiting for him to wake up from his nap and just after his feeding), out into the car, into the car seat, situated with the sun out of his eyes, to grandmother's house for babysitting, out of the car, into the house, out of the warm clothing, diaper changed, comfortable with grandmother and ready for a half day visit could be an exhausting and time-consuming proposition.

The first time they tried to have a romantic "date" together and went through this process, they drove back to their house, went to sleep instead of going "out on the town" and drove back to pick the baby up when the evening was over. They found, over and over again, that they opted to stay home, or one of them stayed home just to make things simpler.

Is this the story of disorganized parents who can't get the situation under control because they are inveterate bumblers? No - this is the story of a man and woman who have begun to lead a very common, and fairly delicate balancing act between caring for their child and finding the time to do other meaningful things in their lives. And this is the story of a couple who have begun to experience a certain detachment in their own relationship as they juggle their new duties.

TIME MANAGEMENT AROUND CHILD CARE ISSUES IS ONE OF THE PRINCIPAL AREAS OF RESENTMENT FOR NEW PARENTS. A MAJOR SOURCE OF DISAPPOINTMENT AND FRUSTRATION FOR NEW PARENTS IS OFTEN THEIR HOPE THAT THEY WILL BE ABLE TO "SQUEEZE" IN THE TIME FOR CREATIVE, PERSONAL PURSUITS. THIS IS USUALLY NOT AS EASY AS IT FIRST APPEARS.

Where does the time come from to have a baby, a career, friends and a continuing couple relationship? Some folks manage just fine; for them it all fits together with ease. We need to know their methods, because even if we don't care to use them ourselves, we will surely meet others along the way who are eager for information about how to put more hours into their parenting days.

Even if the daily and weekly tasks could be organized "just so," the sense of fragmentation that new parents feel can be a source of conflict. Wouldn't it seem that you could visit with a neighbor for an hour while your baby sleeps? But if you do that, when will you prepare the baby's food or wash the clothes or clean up the mess that was made in the morning? Not to mention, when will you do any of the errands that you are normally in charge of, even if you don't have a child? Just how well does it work to sneak your baby's napping hours for your own work, only to be interrupted by cries from the nursery or the sound of little feet in the hall? Can you really be creative and productive (and relaxed?) if you're distracted every ten or fifteen minutes?

notes/thoughts/ideas
talk to. . .
ask about. . .

> *Lynne and Wallace were caught in the "time bind." Wallace went to work every day at a job in another town while Lynne stayed home with the baby. Lynne was a talented artist. She had been a nationally recognized painter since .her teenage years, and now she imagined that there would be the time to continue her life's work. They built a studio in the house, set p the tools of her trade, and waited for her to get the ball rolling after Melissa was born. After all, the baby was sleeping much of the day, and Lynne didn't have a thing to do during those hours. Right? Wrong.*

> *When Wallace came home from work, he couldn't understand what Lynne did all day. They were depending on income from her work as an artist, and it was important to both of them that she continue to expand her career. He felt that he was doing everything he could to help her make it happen, and yet she just didn't seem to have the motivation or the drive to get the show on the road.*

> *Even worse, Lynne was depressed about her lack of ability to get back to her work. She talked about it, yet the hours slipped by. Some days she slept all afternoon while the baby was sleeping, other days she spent reading - but it all made her uneasy. She felt unproductive and knew she was letting Wallace down while he was encouraging her to blossom as an artist.*

Coming to grips with these perceptions of how you spend your time during the day and, most important, how you are feeling about your activities and the time it takes to do them, is a vital step in reducing partnership resentments that may crop up during childcare years. Often an "outsider" will see your time management problems better than you do. Taking your partner into your confidence about your conflicts in this area is a very important stage in increasing intimacy.

Rearranging priorities and schedules can be (and has to be) a joint proposition. Both partners can offer advice and solutions, and both partners need to air their feelings about how changes will affect their own particular time "status quo" of needs, expectations and time requirements.

RECOGNIZING THAT <u>YOUR</u> SOLUTION MAY BE YOUR PARTNER'S GREATEST FEAR IS THE BEGINNING OF REDUCING CONFUSION AND CREATING UNDERSTANDING.

TIME PIES

A time pie can help you see just what is happening with the hours in your day. It can be surprising to discover how much time is spent on such activities as sleeping, running errands or child care. If you have frequent debates about who does what and for how much time, this exercise will give you a black and white picture of how it was, how it is, and how you want it to be.

When you work with the following "time pies" avoid using them as ammunition against your mate. Try to adopt an air of openness and interest as you look at the "time facts." For example, instead of leaping to the front with "See! I told you that you only spend ten minutes a day with the children!" try saying "How do you feel about that time with the children? Is it more or less than you thought it would be? Do you want to make that time block any different? How can I help?" Likewise, you will be surprised at some of your inconsistencies between how you thought you were spending your time and the reality of what you were actually doing. Concentrate on being glad to have this new information and take the stance "Where do we go from here?"

LOOK AT THE EXAMPLE BELOW OF A "TIME PIE":

This time pie was drawn by Paul, the primary "at home" parent for two children. Paul's wife, Susan, worked full time and commuted one hour daily.

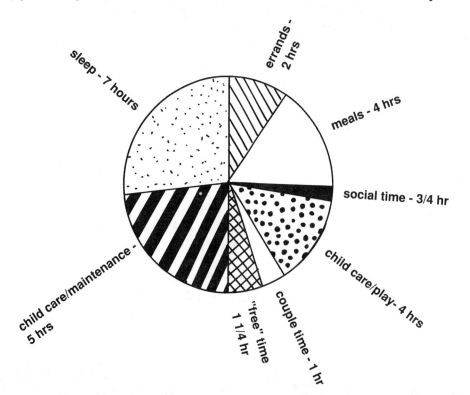

FILL OUT THE TIME PIES BELOW (WRITE IN YOUR ACTIVITIES):

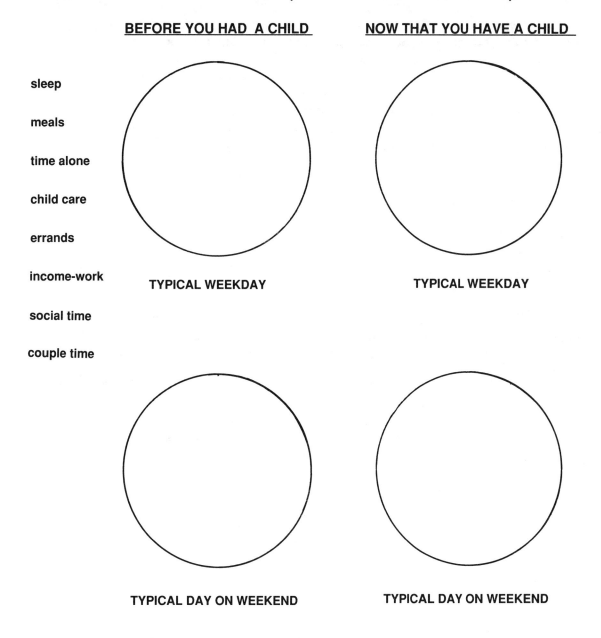

BEFORE YOU HAD A CHILD   NOW THAT YOU HAVE A CHILD

notes/thoughts/ideas
talk to. . .
ask about. . .

sleep

meals

time alone

child care

errands

income-work

social time

couple time

TYPICAL WEEKDAY   TYPICAL WEEKDAY

TYPICAL DAY ON WEEKEND   TYPICAL DAY ON WEEKEND

73

HOW DO YOU SPEND YOUR TIME?

notes/thoughts/ideas
talk to. . .
ask about. . .

1. Are you surprised when you see on paper how you spend your hours during the day? Which areas are larger than you would have guessed? Which are smaller?

2. Number the areas that you would like to change from 1 to 5 in order of importance to you. Talk with your partner about why these changes might be difficult for personal (or other) reasons. What are your fears? What are your hopes?

3. Are you surprised at your partner's time pie? What is different from what you would have expected?

4. Trading time pies - mark in red the amount of time that you wish your partner would "take over" for you in your time pie. Don't be concerned about whether or not you think this could actually happen - just work according to your wishes.

5. Talk with your partner about changes that can happen. Start small. Could it change for a week, just to see the difference? What would you be willing to do to help your partner adjust his or her time pie?

6. Talk to friends and family about solutions to time problems. How have they worked out schedules and the breakdown of activities in their partnerships?

**LOOK AT YOUR RESPONSES FROM THE PREVIOUS PAGE.
CONSIDER THE FOLLOWING QUESTIONS AND SHARE YOUR THOUGHTS
AND FEELINGS WITH YOUR PARTNER.**

1. How can you rearrange your hours so that you have more time together as a couple? What feelings does the prospect of "more time with my partner" bring to the surface?

_____ excitement		_____ apprehension
_____ anxiety		_____ joy
_____ disbelief		_____ pleasure
_____ dullness		_____ caution

2. Close your eyes and create a mental image of you and your partner spending time alone as a couple. Where would you be? What would you be doing? What would you be saying to each other? What feelings would you have?

3. Do you know couples who are so accustomed to spending time separately they can't imagine what they would do if they <u>were</u> given that time as a couple? Are you such a pair?

4. List three non-stressful ways that you and your partner could spend more time together.

  1.

  2.

  3.

5. Will you do it? Why not? Who can help you? Will you let them?

TIME <u>THEN</u> AND TIME <u>NOW</u> AS A COUPLE

notes/thoughts/ideas
talk to. . .
ask about. . .

Use information from the "time pies" on the previous pages to fill out the following charts.

Before We Had A Child	Now That We have A Child
We spent time <u>as a couple</u> doing:	We spend time <u>as a couple</u> doing:
1.	1.
2.	2.
3.	3.
<u>As a couple</u>, we liked to:	<u>As a couple</u>, we like to:
1.	1.
2.	2.
3.	3.
<u>We made the time</u> to be together by:	<u>We make the time</u> to be together by:
1.	1.
2.	2.
3.	3.

ASK YOUR FRIENDS AND FAMILY WHAT HAPPENED TO THEIR TIME AS A COUPLE AFTER THEY BECAME PARENTS. WHAT DO THEY WISH THEY HAD DONE DIFFERENTLY? WHAT IS THEIR ADVICE TO YOU?

MYTH NUMBER THREE
I'M (WE'RE) WAITING UNTIL WE HAVE TIME
TO DEAL WITH THIS

Procrastination in the area of human interaction is a subject that you'll need to meet head-on. Procrastination (putting off 'til tomorrow what should be done today) usually rises from a fund of fears and insecurities. Waiting for the perfect time can indicate a fear of success and a tie with failure. There is always the time to do what we want and need to do. The question is never "<u>is</u> there time?," but rather "<u>when</u> will we make time?"

1. **Are you secretly hoping to run out of time? What are the conflicting feelings that you have about staying in your relationship? How are they affecting your ability to move toward solutions?**

2. **What are you afraid of?**

3. **What are the small steps that you can take to get things moving?**

4. **Say the following statement to yourself, "There will never be a better time to start getting closer and start resolving our conflicts." How does saying this make you feel?**

5. **What is worst thing that can happen if you start today?**

CHAPTER FOUR

MUSING

YOU'RE JUST LIKE YOUR MOTHER. . .

Depending on your point of view, a statement such as "You're just like your mother. . ." can be music to your ears, or represent fighting words. For most men and women, the process of growing away from parents and rejecting their values and interests is an important one. It's a natural part of how we emerge as individuals and set the tone for our own life directions. But until we get to that time of acceptance when we have integrated our parents' histories with our own, we can expect to have immense anxiety about "being like them. "

notes/thoughts/ideas
talk to. . .
ask about. . .

When you're twenty, you might say:

I'm so glad I'm not like my mother, she's very_____ and I'm not! I'll never be like that!

The rest of the message is:

I can sure see the inefficient and unpleasant way my mother acts, and I know that I want to be different. I' m a good example of someone who has learned from their parents' mistakes.

When you're thirty, you might be saying:

Boy, that was a strange thing I said. I sounded just like my father!

The rest of the message is:

Uh, oh. I still have a little bit of potential for acting (or talking or. . .) like my father. It's a good thing that I'm aware of it, so I can nip it in the bud!

When you're forty, you might be saying:

I can understand why my mother (or father) said that (or acted like that.)

The rest of the message is:

Now that I've been through some rough times, I'm not so hard on her (or him). Now I can see how she (or he) got to be that way, and I've got some compassion for them!

Patsy told the following story about attempting to reconcile the idea of being like her mother:

"One day, I was so frazzled by all I had to get done that I found myself screaming at the top of my lungs at my three-year old son. I was completely out of control. Suddenly I heard my voice and it sounded like my mother yelling at us when we were kids - we always described it as a screaming banshee!

My husband, Jack came running into the room and I was mortified. I thought for sure he would tell me to calm down and get a hold of myself. But, instead he put his arms around me and said, 'Patsy, it's okay. No wonder you're upset - it's been a long day. And, by the way, you don't sound anything like your mother.'

At that point, I hadn't said a word about my horror at hearing my mother's strained voice coming out of <u>me,</u> but he knew it was a sensitive subject for me and wanted to reassure me right away. There was something about the way he did it that let me know he was on my side - that he wasn't waiting for me to "blow it" as a parent. To tell you the truth, after that I was a lot more relaxed about my ability to be a good mother and not be tripped up by my past."

How does it happen that we can change our view of our parents so drastically over the course of many years? How does it happen that we can end up acting like our parents when we have fought so vehemently against that very end?

There is a way to examine this dilemma that may provide some illumination. If you are like most people, you lack information about what your parents were like when they were in their teens or twenties. Unless you heard family stories, you can't be sure how they acted, what they did with their days or nights, and exactly what their personal relationships were like. Yes, of course, you often hear the 'highlights' of their years, but the subtleties that ran as themes through their lives (and that coax <u>you </u>to be like your parents in basic ways) are usually missing.

"What do you think? Are you just like your mother too? How did that happen to both of us?"

Take the sting out of the observation that you may be much like your mother or father by noticing how they grew and changed throughout their lives, moving from childhood to adulthood. The better you understand how your own history is interwoven with that of your parents', the better able you will be to make conscious decisions that will lead you in directions that <u>you</u> want to go. Never dismiss the possibility that, as you grow older, you will understand some of your parents' perspectives that were foreign to you as a young adult. You may <u>then</u> choose alternate avenues that you would not think of now. **The goal is not to find solutions for becoming more or less like your parents, but to recognize the potential for following them that lies within you.**

1. Do you know how <u>your</u> parents wanted to be the same or different from their parents?

2. How do your siblings see your mother and father? How are <u>their</u> perspectives different from your own? How do you explain these differences?

3. What are your "big" issues when thinking of your parents? Does your partner know the ways in which you strive to be the same or different from your parents? How can he or she help you feel comfortable with this part of your life? Share these thoughts with your partner.

83

WHAT DO YOU KNOW ABOUT YOUR PARENTS
WHEN THEY WERE YOUNGER?

notes/thoughts/ideas
talk to. . .
ask about. . .

Fill out the time lines below. Use ten year segments as your time guides. You might want to identify such themes as years of childbearing, illness, family moves, or school years.

Notice the similarities and dissimilarities over the years between you and your parents. Think in terms of life style, values, relationships, fears, hopes and dreams.

Share your thoughts with your partner and hear about his or her parents' history.

mother

father

me

84

FILL OUT THE FOLLOWING CHART.

notes/thoughts/ideas
talk to. . .
ask about. . .

**I want to be like my mother
in these ways:**

_____

_____

_____

_____

**I don't want to be like my mother
in these ways:**

_____

_____

_____

_____

**I want to be like my father
in these ways:**

_____

_____

_____

_____

**I don't want to be like my father
in these ways:**

_____

_____

_____

_____

**NOW PUT A STAR NEXT TO THE STATEMENTS THAT DESCRIBE HOW
YOU SEE YOURSELF.** Would other people describe you the same way?
Would your partner?

MY PARENTS AS PARENTS

notes/thoughts/ideas
talk to. . .
ask about. . .

Of course, new parents come to the role with expectations about how they will do their "job." You will have specific areas, drawn from your own upbringing, in which you will wish to emulate or discard your parents' actions. There will probably be ways you would like to parent just like your own parents did, and ways in which you want to be totally different. Deciding that either of these scenarios is possible will mean that you have, once again, taken a clear look at what is influencing you and your partner. This perspective will greatly enhance your chance of giving each other the support you need in your new family.

WRITE DOWN THE PLUSES AND MINUSES OF YOUR PARENTS' PARENTING STYLES. CIRCLE THE ITEMS THAT YOU HOPE TO DO DIFFERENTLY NOW THAT <u>YOU</u> ARE A PARENT.

How are your concerns similar or dissimilar to those of your partner?

pluses	minuses

THINK ABOUT THIS: DID YOU CHOOSE YOUR PARTNER BECAUSE HE OR SHE COULD HELP YOU BE THE KIND OF PARENT THAT IS YOUR IDEAL? IS YOUR PARTNER SIMILAR OR DISSIMILAR TO YOUR OWN PARENTS ON "HOT" TOPICS FOR YOU? WHAT PROBLEMS OR SOLUTIONS DID THIS CHOICE OF CO-PARENT BRING TO YOUR LIFE? NOW THAT YOU HAVE MADE YOUR CHOICE, HOW CAN YOU CONTINUALLY IMPROVE YOUR CHANCES OF WORKING TOGETHER?

CONSPIRACY OF SILENCE -
WHY DIDN'T SOMEBODY TELL US?

notes/thoughts/ideas
talk to. . .
ask about. . .

Whenever new parents are together, you can expect to hear stories about diapers, child care, first steps taken and first words spoken. Along with these stories of delight in the new baby, you are almost guaranteed to be in on a passel of tales that start out with "Why didn't somebody tell us. . .?" Why didn't somebody tell them? Tell them what? What is it that new parents are wishing that someone had told them about being a parent? If you listen closely you'll hear all the questions that parents have - that they think someone (their own parents? their neighbors? books? television?) could have explained in greater detail, with a little more honesty.

You may also notice that these conversations often don't stop with just wishing for more information. Some men and women feel so short-changed by the lack of "real" information they were given about the experience of parenthood that they actually seem to think that other parents are participating in a conspiracy of silence.

Does this sound absurd? Can anyone <u>really</u> be imagining that other people are keeping vital information from them that might make their road a bit easier as they make this dramatic life transition - from couplehood to parenthood?

An evening at a neighborhood party left both Michelle and her best friend Barbara reeling with the thought that their parents hadn't told them enough about what to expect when they became new parents. Everyone at the party talked about how much more was involved than they had been led to expect. Not only the nine months, of course, and the two or three months "recouping" time afterwards, but the hours everyday that would have to go into babycare. The neighbors all shared their dismay at the sheer amount of time it took to get things done - it seemed to be a never-ending set of tasks, and they felt exhausted.

At first Michelle was disgusted with the conversation. She felt that the people who were complaining seemed incredibly naive about the tasks of being a parent. But then she heard Barbara chiming in with her own version of the story, and listened a little more carefully.

87

Michelle and Barbara had babies within one month of each other. All through their teen years they had fantasized about the time when they would be dropping off their children at each others' houses for the day while they went off to visit with friends and neighbors. The reality was that Barbara felt too overwhelmed by being a new mother to spend many hours "out on the town" with friends. She stayed at home and spent a lot of time aimlessly reading and cleaning, feeling left out of the mainstream of her friends' lives, but without the energy to do anything about it.

After the party, Michelle and Barbara began to share other stories about the changes that new parenthood had brought to their lives. There was the joy of taking care of a baby and seeing this small being grow from day to day. But there was also the reality of too little time to be a couple with the "new dad" and a serious lack of intimacy in their sexual relationships. For Michelle this was a far more important problem than "time to get things done." She saw her relationship with her husband slipping away, and didn't know how to bring it back to life.

As they talked about these changes, Michelle and Barbara wondered how many other people felt the same way. But even more, they began to wonder why no one they knew had "warned" them that their lives might change so dramatically once they had a child. What started as an afternoon "gab" session turned into an intense period of trying to remember just what they had been told before they became parents - what was the news that other parents had given them?

"When you said that at the party I couldn't believe it. I didn't know you were having trouble, too."

TRADING INFORMATION - WHY IT'S IMPORTANT

Most men and women <u>can</u> remember the themes that their friends and relatives brought home about being a parent. The refrain that "Your life is really going to change once you have a baby" is pretty common. That message goes winging back and forth between friends and generations all the time. But <u>how</u> are their lives going to change? And, most important of all, are there some changes that go beyond the stresses of common parenting and the sharing of lives with a new baby that require a greater effort on the part of the information-bearer to pass along?

As an example, news about Postpartum Depression is typical of the type of information that is vital to the well-being of new families. Yet there is a dismal track record for raising community consciousness when it comes to taking "post-pregnancy blues" seriously. For decades, a significant number of women have experienced mild to severe depression after the birth of a child. For some, it's been a case of

crying jags that come from nowhere, a sense of helplessness (or hopelessness). For others it has bee
an experience fraught with paranoia and deep despair which may lead to violence, and in extreme cas
imperil the health and life of the new mother and her baby.

With an experience that provokes such confusion and disharmony in an individual and her family, and strikes with such frequency (statistics tell us that as many as one in ten new mothers actually have the symptoms of "psychosis", a breaking away from reality after birth, and many many more experience a lesser but still disturbing depression) it's hard to believe that this subject is rarely talked about. How is it that women routinely regard postpartum adjustment as an experience that should be hidden (Does it mean I'm an unfit mother? Has something gone terribly wrong with my mind?) and dealt with on a private or purely familial basis? Can you remember someone in your family, or your neighborhood (are we talking about you or your partner?) having a sense of depression after the birth of a child that seemed to defy all attempts at alleviation?

If you know of such a case (or cases) what did you surmise from the facts that you were given? Did you think of the Postpartum Depression as an indication of something gone awry with the new mother? Was it an indication of her poor skills at handling stress? Did it give you answers about her childhood or poor relationships in the past that had never been resolved and were surfacing as depression and psychosis? With a surface knowledge of this common dilemma, any of these possibilities might be seen as valid.

FOR THOSE OF THE PSYCHIATRIC AND MEDICAL PROFESSION WHO HAVE STUDIED THIS PHENOMENON THERE IS NO MYSTERY AND THE ANSWERS LIE NOT IN THE PSYCHOLOGY, BUT THE PHYSIOLOGY OF THE NEW MOTHER. POSTPARTUM DEPRESSION AND PSYCHOSIS ARE TRIGGERED BY THE NATURAL EBB AND FLOW OF THE HORMONES IN A WOMAN'S BODY THAT GEAR UP DURING PREGNANCY AND DRASTICALLY GEAR DOWN AFTER THE BIRTH. THE SAME SYMPTOMS THAT OCCUR IN ANY MAN OR WOMAN WITH A DEPLETION OF CORTISONE, PROGESTERONE OR THYROID IN THE SYSTEM ARE THE SYMPTOMS THAT ACCOMPANY POSTPARTUM DEPRESSION.

So here we have a prime example of how some men and women come to view a lack of information about pregnancy and parenting as a "conspiracy of silence" against new parents. And it comes not only from friends and neighbors who do not see the value in sharing their stories and offering personal support for others, but from a society that is just beginning to learn to care about the "problems" that women face and delve into their causes and cures. Information about Postpartum Depression is crucial to positive adjustment for many new parents. It goes miles in reducing blame for stress and strain in a new family, and yet all around us these stories of depression are almost "secrets" as mothers struggle to understand the changes that are going on psychologically and physiologically within them. Isn't this the kind of information that couples and parents should be passing on to others: information that tells of questions and answers and, most of all, natural transition and ways to cope.

"I wonder why Jan never told us they had so many problems with their marriage after the baby came. . ."

As we discuss the various types of information that others might be interested in relating to new parents, there is the oft-present question that arises, about "telling too much." Will you discourage people if you "come on too strong"? What are the possibilties for helping new parents be better prepared for the changes that parenting will bring to their lives? Will anyone listen if you tell them? Can you pass on your own stories with the right degree of balance between the joys and the frustrations, the questions and the answers? If you wish to pave the way for others, is there the danger that you are <u>just</u> telling your own story - a story that will have no relevance for others, and may confuse them or even cause them to question your intent in "telling"?

Can anyone who has not actually experienced parenting ever <u>really</u> understand all that is being communicated? I think not. New parents often wish to find out for themselves. Many imagine that whatever the experience of others, theirs will certainly be substantially different. Of course in many cases this will be true. For an equal number of people, however, the responses they have to parenting will be quite similar to the ones experienced by the message-bearers many months before. Those parents may have tried to give an inside look at their own transition to parenthood, but, unfortunately, the message may not have been delivered in the right words, or the right tone, or at the right time.

USE THE NEXT EXERCISES TO LOOK AT THE WAYS YOU HAVE GAINED INFORMATION ABOUT PARENTING

90

INFORMATION FROM OTHER PARENTS

WHAT DO YOU REMEMBER THAT OTHER PARENTS TOLD YOU ABOUT PREGNANCY, CHILDBIRTH AND CHILDREARING?

notes/thoughts/ideas
talk to. . .
ask about. . .

1.

2.

3.

4.

5.

Did you believe them? Do you believe them now?

Did you understand what they were saying? Now do you understand?

Were you glad to get the information?

Did you question their motivation in telling you?

Did you feel that you didn't want to know what they were saying? That you
wanted it to be <u>your</u> experience and didn't want to be influenced by others
and <u>their</u> experience? Do you feel any differently now?

91

HAVE YOU EVER THOUGHT THAT OTHER PARENTS (PERHAPS YOUR OWN?) DIDN'T GIVE YOU THE REAL SCOOP ON BEING A PARENT, THAT THEY WITHHELD INFORMATION?

List the areas or issues where you could have used help:

1.

2.

3.

4.

5.

In each of the areas above, what do <u>you</u> now know that you can pass on to others who are new parents?

THE PASSING ON OF STORIES CAN HELP US ALL UNDERSTAND THE COMMONALITY OF LIFE TRANSITION. LEARNING TO USE OUR ELDERS AS RESOURCES WILL GIVE US PRACTICE FOR THE TIME WHEN <u>WE</u> ARE THE ELDERS, AND OTHERS WILL BE LOOKING TO US FOR STRENGTH AND KNOWLEDGE AND INSPIRATION.

MYTH NUMBER FOUR
SOMETIMES PEOPLE GET ALONG SO WELL THEY DON'T HAVE ANY MYSTERY OR EXCITEMENT LEFT IN THEIR RELATIONSHIP.

It doesn't take too many negative associations before men and women (and children) start to pair up "conflict" and "love." In many families, they go hand in hand. This familiarity with conflict and sometimes fear and the expression of love, can cause us to doubt the value of relationships that do not have such stressors as their foundation. We will all have problems for which we will have to find solutions, but continual conflict is more than just problem-solving - it is also wears down the reserves of the people involved.

notes/thoughts/ideas
talk to. . .
ask about. . .

1. Do you know a couple who get along so well that their relationship is dry and boring? How do they live? How are their values and ideas similar to yours? How are they different? What have you learned from observing them?

2. Do you know a couple who has an exciting relationship, yet one that is relatively conflict-free? How do they live? How are their values and ideas similar to yours? How are they different? What have you learned from observing them?

3. Does your partnership thrive on the artificial excitement of conflict?

4. Have you known a couple whose relationship has improved over many, many years? What do you know about the subtleties of their interaction? Ask them how they have stayed intimate with each other. What did you learn from talking to them?

CHAPTER FIVE

STRUGGLING

SHOULDN'T WE BE ABLE TO FIGURE THIS OUT OURSELVES?

Like many families, many couples strongly believe that people should always be able to work out problems without help from the "outside world." It can be seen as a sign of weakness to tell others what is bothering you. Some people are shamed by neighbors knowing (or guessing) that members of the family are going through difficult times. So, if you aren't going to let on that you are troubled, if no one knows the kind of problem you are having or the intensity of the feelings that go with it, who will be inclined to pass on assistance in the form of shared stories and real information that may lead to solutions? Where will you ever get advice and suggestions from those who have experienced similar concerns?

notes/thoughts/ideas
talk to. . .
ask about. . .

IN YEARS PAST, IT WASN'T SUCH A DIFFICULT QUESTION

When families lived in one place for many years (and even many generations) their roots tended to grow down deep. There was a storyline that flowed naturally from the elders to the youngers and around the neighborhood. Mr. Jones down the street could tell you that your great-great grandparents had had some of the same problems when they were first married. Mrs. Schwartz, who knew you since you were five, could feel quite comfortable offering suggestions now that you were thirty-five. The whole community might pull together to help a family in distress - connections were clear and bonding among friends and neighbors was expected.

But times have changed. The average American family moves every five years - and these changes of residence have more impact on the cultural and social and psychological heritage of couples and families than we might guess. With parents and other elders and family members often many miles away, it isn't easy to find a confidante and informal advisor to help with couple difficulties or to answer common questions about the many facets of child-rearing. One response to the lack of familial

"I want to share this part of your mother's journal with you. She wrote it when you were very young. We were feeling overwhelmed, too."

97

connection has been the growth of a people-service industry that offers professional counseling assistance to those in need. In recent years both men and women have turned in large numbers to counselors, therapists and other human service professionals to get help in answering questions about their lives and relationships. And now, communities have found ways to assist those who cannot afford (or do not care to enter into) individual and couple counseling. In many areas of the country there are "self-help" groups and classes to help us all gain information and support for any number of difficulties.

Still, there is a limit to the information that people routinely pass on about how they are making it or have made it through major life transitions. Pregnancy and child rearing are cases in point. Very often neither men nor women know what other couples are experiencing. They aren't sure what the problems are with which other couples may be dealing, and they may not know what others are doing to arrive at solutions.

New parenting can be an isolating experience. It takes hope and courage to try out new roles in the world, and it takes a different kind of hope and courage to learn from others who have gone before. We may have a stake in believing that our problem is unique - that no one else has ever felt the same way or been saddled with the same set of insurmountable circumstances. In some ways this is true - we are each unique in the way we approach life situations, and in the way life creates its own special package of assets and liabilities for us to examine. But, on the other hand, life transitions have fairly common themes. We all experience birth, tragedy, happiness, and death. Change is part of every human life, and all around us are people who have traveled the same road we are traveling now. They may have done better or worse, but they all have news to pass on.

Carl and Liz each came from families where all problems were kept strictly at home. Their parents were horrified when the children told neighbors about disagreements in the family. Both Carl and Liz found that, as adults, they were embarrassed to let others know they were having any difficulties adjusting to being new parents.

Carl felt that if his colleagues knew about his home-life problems they would be put off - they would see him as "unstable" and "weak." Liz was afraid to talk to close friends and be seen as a complainer. She felt she wasn't making the same satisfactory adjustment to parenting that her mother and sisters had and, as a result, felt guilty.

A standstill in the making, but luckily for them, a close friend who had a two-year old daughter made the effort to sit down over dinner and talk about his own experiences. Mack and his wife showed up at the house one night quite spontaneously. Mack talked about his insecurities as a new father, his arguments with his wife over money, and the

98

classes they were attending where a large group of people traded ideas and patted each other on the back for trying to remain a couple, even after having a child. As he described it, in these classes it seemed that someone always had an idea for someone else's problem - there was a give and take that uplifted everybody and encouraged everyone present to try their hand at helping out.

Mack let Carl and Liz know that, in the beginning, he was scared of what he had taken on as a father. He was frightened of reliving some of the parts of his own growing-up that he didn't like. His father was an alcoholic, his mother a quiet woman who was distraught most of Mack's school years. The family was tense - there was rarely any laughter and drama was the name of the game. Every life situation turned into a circus and free-for-all that amplified the feelings out of proportion and created a sense of theatrical unreality about everyday problems.

As a new parent, Mack worried about everything, and watched his marriage teeter on the brink of disaster more than once as his wife, Susan, struggled with her own adjustments to being a new mother. One day while he was sitting in the yard, staring off into space, wondering what the escape route should be, his ninety year old neighbor walked by and sat down for a chat.

"I want to thank you and your wife for coming over to the house and talking to us. It helped - we've been feeling pretty hopeless lately."

Frank's visit was the turning point for both Mack as a parent and for Mack and Susan as a couple. This man, who had lived for nine decades, told his own marriage stories that had Mack laughing, on the verge of crying, and recognizing himself in every other tale. Frank had been married for over seventy years and he had a wealth of ideas on how to smooth things over, how to come up with new solutions, how to make things work and still be in love. That first day was the start of a long friendship between Mack and Frank - they spent hours trading histories, and now Mack was passing on the favor to Carl and Liz.

WHERE DID YOU GET <u>YOUR</u> MESSAGES
ABOUT ASKING FOR HELP?

notes/thoughts/ideas
talk to. . .
ask about. . .

LOOK AT THE FOLLOWING LIST OF "MESSAGE BEARERS."
FILL OUT THE CHART INDICATING THEIR IDEAS ABOUT ASKING FOR
HELP FROM OTHERS.

Message bearer	The Message Was:		How did this work for them?
	Do it alone	Ask for help	
Mother			
Father			
Grandparents			
Brothers			
Sisters			
Teacher			
Neighbor			
Friends			

AND WHAT ABOUT YOU? ARE YOU OUT OF PERSONAL RESOURCES? IS IT TIME TO
TRUST OTHERS AND TURN TO THEM FOR CREATIVE SOLUTIONS?

WHO'S ON YOUR SIDE?

On the following page you will find words that describe issues that frequently affect people's lives. Unless you are very unusual these issues will have relevance for you, too. Take time to consider all of these issues in light of being a new parent. Add your own topics to the list.

Think of all of the people in your life who care for and influence you.

They are the "message bearers" who hold keys for moving through life's doors. They have questions and answers and stories to help you make a smoother transition. You might be including grandparents, neighbors, doctors, teachers, classmates, sisters and brothers and work colleagues. You and your partner are included in this group, as you serve as resources for each other and for others you know.

Draw a circle around each issue and consider what "resource" person in your life is the most connected to this issue. This might be because of their own experience, a story they have told you, advice they have given you, or something you have observed about the way they live their lives.

Write the name of the "resource" person in the circle with the issue.

Why did you make these associations?

2. **Are these people you feel comfortable talking to?**

3. **Have you already asked them for information about these topics?**
   If not, why not?

4. **Make an effort in the next days to write to or talk to these people and hear their stories. Ask them, especially, how these topics changed for them after they became parents and what advice they would pass on to other parents looking for answers.**

101

TRUST

Fear of Love

Child Care

discipline

Fear of Failure

PHYSICAL AFFECTION

career concerns

PARENTING WORRIES

fatigue

anger/bitterness

Fear of Death

MONEY WORRIES

sexuality

fear of rejection

Relaxation and Leisure Time

JEALOUSY

102

YOU WLL NOTICE THAT PEOPLE EVERYWHERE ARE YEARNING TO HAVE WARM, INTIMATE CONTACT WITH FAMILY AND FRIENDS. MANY PEOPLE ALSO WANT TO HAVE CHILDREN AND ADD THAT DIMENSION OF STRENGTH AND CLOSENESS TO THEIR WORLD. IT ISN'T ALWAYS EASY TO FIGURE OUT HOW TO HELP A COUPLE WHO HAVE BECOME PARENTS HAVE A PARTNERSHIP THAT WILL LAST THE MANY YEARS OF A LIFETIME.

BUT WE ARE ALL ON THE SAME SIDE, AND WE CAN ALL PROVIDE THE ENCOURAGEMENT TO MAKE IT HAPPEN.

IS IT
COMPETITION OR COMMUNICATION?

When you talk to your partner are you competing or communicating? On the left side of this page are "awareness questions" used by a tennis coach who specializes in helping players tune into their inner rhythms and messages while they are playing tennis. He asks his players to think about the questions after a match. On the right side of the page are these same questions transformed for partners who are trying to talk together. Which side best reflects <u>your</u> attitude and approach?

notes/thoughts/ideas
talk to. . .
ask about. . .

How did I feel in the warm-up? as the match began?	**How did I feel before we began to talk? As we began to talk?**
Was I confident about winning the match?	**Was I confident that I could communicate my feelings and listen well?**
Were my muscles tense during the match?	**Were my muscles tense while we were talking?**
What was I thinking about when I was playing well? poorly?	**What was I thinking about when we were communicating well? Poorly?**
How and why did my breathing change during the match?	**How and why did my breathing change while we were talking?**
What happened to make me angry or frustrated? Did I play better or worse?	**What happened to make me angry or frustrated? Did I communicate better or worse?**
What happened to make me feel happy, confident and energized?	**What happened to make me feel happy, confident and energized?**
How was I affected by the score?	**Did I feel that he or she "won" or "lost"?**
How did the final outcome of the match compare with my initial feelings of winning or losing?	**How did the final outcome of the conversation compare wih my initial feelings?**

105

GUILT:
THE PARENT MERRY-GO-ROUND

Guilt is our way of "staying in line" with the messages we have gotten over the years about what is right or wrong. Guilt can live so deep within us that sometimes we aren't even clearly aware of why we are feeling bad about what we are doing. Actions that seem like run-of-the-mill responses to daily life can inspire feelings of self-hatred and self-recrimination. If you grew up in a family where there were many "shoulds" and "shouldn'ts," you may have a difficult time knowing when you are acting out of guilt. If you have a very stern approach to life, with quite a structured system for evaluating the rights and wrongs or "goodness" or badness" of the events around you, guilt may also be a frequent emotion for you.

Guilt can also be a measure of how well you are living up to your own values and expectations. But there is always the question - are these your values or are they someone else's? Take the time to evaluate these messages and determine how relevant (or accurate) they are for your current situation. In other words, it is important to update your personal information bank, and decide if the opinions you're hanging onto still serve you well.

Since guilt can permeate all facets of our life, don't imagine that subjects such as pregnancy and child rearing (and the birth itself) can get away without it. Guilt around these issues comes at new parents from all directions. As you bob and weave to establish your own firm footing, take a look at the very common guilt inducers listed on the next pages. Those who love you would probably not describe themselves as being on a mission to make you anxious, but their hints and ideas and concerns about your ways of being a parent may have some pretty sharp barbs and hidden messages tagging along.

FILL OUT THE CHARTS ON THE FOLLOWING PAGES.
Check which people have given you these messages.
Put a star in the "ME" column if you've said this to someone else.
Don't forget to laugh if some of these items stretch the boundaries of
  credibility for you and your partner!

PREGNANCY GUILT

notes/thoughts/ideas
talk to. . .
ask about. . .

THE PREGNANCY	mother	father	grand parents	in-laws	neighbors/ friends	me
Alcohol during pregnancy						
Smoking during pregnancy						
Gained too much weight						
Didn't gain enough weight						
Didn't get enough exercise						
Got the wrong kind of exercise						
Ate the wrong foods						
Angry during pregnancy						
Slept too much						
Didn't have right "layette"						
Made love during pregnancy						
Exposed to German measles						
Depressed during pregnancy						
Didn't have the "maternal glow"						
Had stretch marks						

MORE GUILT - THIS TIME ABOUT THE BIRTH

THE BIRTH ITSELF	mother	father	grand parents	in-laws	neighbors/ friends	me
Labor took too long						
Needed medication for pain						
Didn't attend childbirth classes						
Didn't have hospital birth						
Hospital birth, not home birth						
Screamed during labor						
Rude to doctors/ nurses/ partner during labor						
Needed episiotomy & stitches						
Caesarean birth						
Partner wasn't at birth						
Baby was breech position						
Didn't get house clean before						
Didn't think the baby was cute						
Was depressed after birth						

notes/thoughts/ideas
talk to. . .
ask about. . .

notes/thoughts/ideas
talk to. . .
ask about. . .

TAKING CARE OF BABY	mother	father	grand parents	in-laws	neighbors/ friends	me
Isn't warm enough						
Too warm						
Cutting the fingernails						
Baby is hungry						
Too thin						
Too fat						
Cradle cap						
Crying too much - colic						
Don't let the baby cry enough						
Boy dressed in pink						
Girl dressed in blue						
Sleeps with parents						
Breastfeeding vs. bottle						
Cat in the baby's room						
Noises too loud around baby						

MORE GUILT! - CHILD CARE

CHILD CARE	mother	father	grand parents	in-laws	neighbors/ friends	me
Plays with food						
Use playpen/childleash						
Father not involved enough						
Cloth diapers vs. paper						
When to start solid foods						
Holding up/walking too soon						
Walking too late						
Toilet training too soon						
Toilet training too late						
Went back to work too soon						
Swimming or not?						
Sucks thumb/carries blanket						
Preschool or not?						
Hair too short for girls/ too long for boys						

notes/thoughts/ideas
talk to. . .
ask about. . .

DO YOU GET THE PICTURE?

notes/thoughts/ideas
talk to. . .
ask about. . .

Do you imagine that couples who are expecting and who have new babies <u>really</u> need the barrage of suggestions and critiques that flow quite spontaneously out of the mouths of every child care expert around (and aren't we <u>all</u> experts on how to take care of someone else's child)?

What about changing this scenario just a bit. Yes, there <u>is</u> information that parents need and yes there <u>are</u> different ways (some better, some worse) of being pregnant and taking care of children. Pass along what you will. After all, that is what this manual is about - giving support and information to others as they go from couplehood to parenthood. But, shine the other side of the coin, too, by remembering that new parents are vulnerable human beings. They are off on a course that is one of the most important in their lives - learning to love their child and give the best care possible on the way to adulthood. And, while they are doing this, they are needing to nurture their own sense of competency and ability to "do it right."

Remember that new parents are often defensive about their roles and expectations. They, like all of us, will listen better and adjust more quickly if they are treated with the respect they deserve for taking on this life challenge. You can help build the self-esteem of your partner (and your friends) by using the following statements to bolster confidence and improve communication.

TRY THESE OUT ON A REGULAR BASIS:

I love the way you _____ with your baby!

Where did you learn to _____? That's a good idea!

You sure have a nice way of _____your baby!

I admire the way you _____.

I respect you for the way you _____.

Can you help me with _____?

Can I help you with _____?

That's a great idea! I'll try that one myself!

STOPPING THE WORD WARS-
TELL ME YOU CARE

It's easy to see that certain ways of saying things - our choice of words and the attitude behind those words - can inspire openness or forgiveness or hope in others. Other ways can cause these same people to close their emotional "doors" to our message and can create an atmosphere of anger or competition that is hard to penetrate.

Using statements that say what you mean yet defuse negative emotionals is crucial in creating good faith and good will. One type of statement that can accomplish this is the "validation" statement. Validation statements succeed in breaking down barriers of anger and confusion. We choose to address our partner with words of encouragement and support for real feelings and achievements and concerns.

Something to think about: habits take a while to change, and if you've developed the habit of speaking in angry, alienating tones, it will not disappear overnight. Nor will your partner necessarily be more appreciative than suspicious when you first begin to try. But you will be surprised at how quickly the habit of being positive will become second nature now that you've begun.

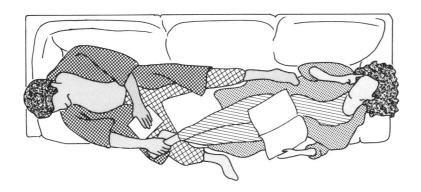

"I know it took a lot of guts to say that, and I appreciate your honesty. It's one of the things I admire about you, even if I feel bad about what you say sometimes."

113

MAKING A DIFFERENCE WITH WORDS

PRACTICE USING THE FOLLOWING PHRASES.

How do you feel when you anticipate the response you will get from your
partner when you start off communication in this way?

**KEEP TRACK OF HOW MANY TIMES IN A DAY YOU USE PHRASES LIKE
THESE:**

I like it when you. . .

I appreciate. . .

I feel good when you. . .

You helped me by. . .

I like you because. . .

I was interested when you said. . .

It felt good to hear you say. . .

I admired you when you. . .

I admired your honesty when you. . .

I am a lot like you when. . .

I'm glad you noticed that. . .

I'm glad I'm with you because. . .

Thanks for. . .

I feel better when. . .

YOU MAKE ME ANGRY!

Anger - it's one of our most powerful emotions. But depending on your sex, your age, your family, your cultural heritage or a number of other variables, it may be easier for you to show your anger, or easier for you to hide it. It's not uncommon to confuse anger and aggression. Depending on your experiences, or lack thereof, you may think that angry thoughts and feelings will always end in violent confrontations. This observation may encourage you to have violent outbursts. On the other hand, it may cause you to deny that you have any angry feelings at all!

One thing is certain - anger is such an important emotion that if it is suppressed, it will affect your ability to experience other, happier, feelings, too. You might imagine unresolved anger as a thick coating that smothers what is going on underneath. It might seem that there isn't anything going on in those deeper layers; the truth is that those feelings are residing under an "overlay" that makes it extra hard for these emotions to surface.

Gracie and Alan came from very different backgrounds. Gracie's parents fought long and hard - they could never discuss their feelings without a physical battle taking place. Gracie grew up fearing confrontation. She never acknowledged her unhappiness with others, because she didn't know what to do next after the initial attempts to express her feelings.

Gracie felt constantly on edge and unable to have any control over her life - she was always afraid that people would be angry with her if she told them what was on her mind. As the years went by, she noticed with alarm that her feelings were beginning to be "blunted." She never got angry, but she never felt really happy either. This was the crux of the problem that began to surface during her relationship with Alan.

Alan grew up in a family where everyone aired their thoughts and feelings. If someone was upset, they were very direct, and angry words often followed. After that, however, things would settle down and there were usually satisfactory solutions found for family dilemmas.

After two years of marriage, Alan was concerned about Gracie's inability to say what was on her mind. At first he thought she was just "low-key," but then he realized that she had many things bothering her that she never spoke about. His friends told him

115

he was crazy when he voiced his suspicions that all was not quite right. "You should live with <u>my</u> wife if you want to have somebody show their feelings!," they would say in amazement.

Alan's uneasiness didn't go away. He saw that Gracie denied her anger when they were arguing, but that it came out later in discussions that had nothing to do with the original topic. When the feeling surfaced, Gracie was unable to talk or she would say things she didn't mean, and be upset for days afterwards.

Gracie and Alan are not atypical in their differing styles of dealing with anger. They're each using what they learned from their own families, and are dismayed by the other's approach. Once again, these different ways of meeting a problem were only variations on a theme during their dating years. But now they're married and have a baby. Now, these issues of when to get angry and what is appropriate in terms of angry behavior, along with hidden fears about this volatile subject, are coming to the forefront.

After many ill-fated attempts to get Gracie to talk about just why she got so enraged during these arguments, Alan decided to talk about his own upbringing instead. He spent time telling Gracie about his family, and why he thought it had been healthy for him to see people getting angry, and then getting over it. He hadn't come from a physically violent background, so he knew that anger and aggression didn't have to go hand-in-hand.

"It's okay for you to yell when you get mad. We all do it! It doesn't mean that we can't get over it later."

Gracie's first reaction to this sharing was stiffness and fear. She was afraid to hear these words about feelings (and especially angry feelings) and confused by the contradiction between Alan's and her family's experiences. She sat in a cold silence, hoping that Alan would give up talking about this subject.

But Gracie was lucky. Alan was genuinely concerned about their relationship and had his own fears that they weren't going to make it, if they couldn't learn to disagree and resolve their differences. He pursued what he knew was important communication for them, and helped Gracie relax by going slowly. When he saw Gracie get tense, he conquered his own tendency to give up. He stroked her hair, asked questions about her family, and showed that he was interested in knowing how he could help arguments de-escalate before they got out of hand. Gracie slowly got the message, and with it gained renewed hope for her marriage.

116

Reflect on your family. Imagine their conversations and their confrontations while you were growing up.

notes/thoughts/ideas
talk to. . .
ask about. . .

Where were you when the arguments were going on? Did you feel responsible for dissension in your family? Why? As a child did you decide that you would never get angry when you got older?

FILL OUT THE CHART ON THIS PAGE.

What are the messages about anger that you've learned from family members?

Examples: It isn't polite to get angry.
When you get angry, you put a burden on others around you.
People who get angry are hysterical and out of control.
People who get angry will become violent.

Family member	Message	Which part of this message do you think sounds like you?
father		
mother		
brother/sister		
aunt/uncle		
grandmother		
grandfather		
stepparent		

ANGER IS COMPLEX - WE LEARN TO DREAD IT OR TO UNDERSTAND IT MAINLY THROUGH OUR EXPERIENCES WHILE GROWING UP. THE MORE WE UNDERSTAND ANGER IN OUR LIVES, THE MORE RELAXED AND ANXIETY-FREE WE WILL BE AS ADULTS.

117

USE THE FOLLOWING SCALE TO CONSIDER HOW YOU APPROACH ANGER.
Remember that anger is a sensitive subject for almost everyone, but it
becomes less so the more we give ourselves "permission" to understand its
place in our lives.

PUT NUMBERS IN THE BLANKS TO INDICATE:

      1 - just like me
      2 - a lot like me
      3 - sometimes like me
      4 - a little like me
      5 - not at all like me

_____ **I worry about getting too angry.**

_____ **I get angry more easily since I've had a child.**

_____ **I can forgive people who get angry at me without just cause.**

_____ **When I get angry, it seems that it's about something different from what
is really going on.**

_____ **I get angry very quickly.**

_____ **As a child I was angry a lot.**

_____ **I feel okay about telling people if they upset me.**

_____ **I can listen to others who are mad at me without wanting to retaliate.**

_____ **Little things make me mad.**

_____ **I can think of times that I've felt better after expressing negative
feelings.**

UNDERSTANDING ANGER - YOUR MOTHER
(OR A MAJOR FEMALE FIGURE IN YOUR LIFE)

1. What words would you use to describe your mother when she was angry or upset?

2. What kind of issues or events made your mother angry?

3. Did you mother feel okay about showing anger?

4. How did your father react to your mother's anger?

5. How did the children in the family react to your mother's anger?

6. When it comes to anger, how are you similar to your mother? How are you different?

7. When it comes to anger, what do you know about your mother's parents?

SHARE YOUR REFLECTIONS WITH YOUR PARTNER

119

UNDERSTANDING ANGER - YOUR FATHER
(OR A MAJOR MALE FIGURE IN YOUR LIFE)

notes/thoughts/ideas
talk to. . .
ask about. . .

1. What words would you use to describe your father when he was angry or upset?

2. What kind of issues or events made your father angry?

3. Did your father feel okay about showing anger?

4. How did your mother react to your father's anger?

5. How did the children in the family react to your father's anger?

6. When it comes to anger, how are you similar to your father? How are you different?

7. When it comes to anger, what do you know about your father's parents?

SHARE YOUR REFLECTIONS WITH YOUR PARTNER

UNDERSTANDING ANGER
YOU AND YOUR FEELINGS

FILL IN THE FOLLOWING BLANKS.

Don't think too long - answer with the first thing that comes to mind.

notes/thoughts/ideas
talk to. . .
ask about. . .

1. When it comes to getting mad, I _____

2. When I get angry, I have a history of _____

3. When it comes to being upset, people who know me well think I _____
_____

4. When it comes to expressing my anger, I _____

5. The feelings that I associate with being angry are _____

6. The thoughts that I associate with being angry are _____

7. The actions that I associate with being angry are _____

8. In my family, I was the one who got angry by _____

9. The person (people) around me who would be most threatened by my getting
   angry are _____

10. The person (people) around me who would be most appreciative of my
    expressing my negative feelings are _____

SHARE YOUR REFLECTIONS WITH YOUR PARTNER

121

LOOKING AT ANGER
THE ASSOCIATIONS WE MAKE WITH BEING ANGRY

USE THE BOXES BELOW TO TRACE YOUR ANGER BACKWARDS.
Start out with a situation that makes you angry now, and see what
   associations you find.
Sometimes you will notice that "angry" becomes "sad" or "frightened" or takes
   on another feeling as you work your way back.

*(example: I'm angry because you won't help with the dishes ⟶ and that reminds me of
when I was growing up and my father would never help my mother with the housework
and that reminds me of feeling scared when my parents fought ⟶ and that reminds me
of feeling scared when my mother cried ⟶ and that reminds me of being afraid of being
alone if my parents were divorced ⟶ and that reminds me of when my parents split up
and we all moved apart).*

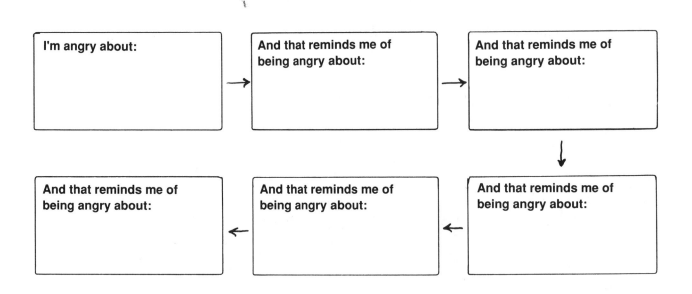

SHARE YOUR THOUGHTS, FEELINGS AND MEMORIES WITH YOUR PARTNER.

MYTH NUMBER FIVE
I NEED A CRISIS TO MOTIVATE ME

Waiting for a crisis before you appreciate the seriousness of a relationship problem is one of the most self-defeating behaviors you can adopt. Sometimes people wait for a crisis to demonstrate to their partner (or family or friends) just how bad it all is. Sometimes they ignore the clues that are building up around them and dive in for the solutions just a little too late. It's a sad mistake to wait until you or your partner are on the edge of despair before you take action. Despite how stalled you may feel, you must be in charge of your ability to get motivated to find solutions. You can begin to find answers at the beginning of the difficulty, or wait until the verdict is in and all that remains is picking up the pieces.

notes/thoughts/ideas
talk to. . .
ask about. . .

1. **Are you crisis-oriented in other aspects of your life? If, not, how do you handle those parts of your life differently?**

2. **What did you learn about relationships and crises from your parents?**

3. **Have you ever taken a course or read a book or heard someone talk about the art of "conflict resolution" (i.e. problem-solving)? Did you know that there are definite techniques that can be applied in business <u>or</u> personal relationships to keep crises to a minimum? What resources are available in your community?**

4. **Say the following statement to yourself - "I do not need a crisis to motivate me. I want to keep my partnership together by listening and acting before it is too late." How did saying that make you feel? What part of you protests the possibility that crisis situations could be eliminated in your life?**

123

CHAPTER SIX

HIDING

DON'T BE AFRAID

Common fears that keep both men and women from exploring new avenues of communication and understanding are such thoughts as:

IF THINGS GET BETTER, WE'LL HAVE TO STAY TOGETHER AND I DON'T REALLY WANT TO.

As issues and tempers get hotter, unconscious decisions may be made to give up on the relationship, even though you say (and may feel) that you are fighting very hard to resolve the differences and stay together. This stance can be tricky - the words are saying one thing, but the actions and the heart may be saying quite another. Attempts to come to agreement may end over and over in bitter stalemate. Underneath the surface of working it all out, there may be strong fears that "working it out" will mean staying together in a relationship that has already been categorized as a "dead issue."

Look closely at this possibility. It is important to realize that getting along better and having less angry feelings (and more understanding) for your partner and the relationship, does not mean having to stay together when "breaking up" is really a better agenda for all concerned.

I'M AFRAID TO BEGIN AGAIN, HAVE NOTHING CHANGE FOR THE BETTER, AND FIND OUT THAT THE RELATIONSHIP REALLY IS HOPELESS.

If you feel that you have tried everything, going to counseling sessions or having serious talks about the future (or doing anything that others think could promote and ignite fears of hopelessness. Especially if you have a

"How can I go back in there and tell her that now I see her point of view?"

history of "failed" relationships, the possibility of actually coming to loving resolution may seem very remote. Geared for the end, you may be afraid to take one more chance, afraid to put fragile feelings

127

back on the line. One more bit of news that nothing can be worked out may seem more than you can bear.

I'M AFRAID THAT EVERYTHING WILL BE REVEALED TO BE MY FAULT. I'LL BE EXPOSED AS THE PERSON OF BLAME FOR ALL OF THE DIFFICULTIES.
Tender feelings of guilt and confusion about the role that they have played in the problems of the relationship may cause couples to be especially wary of such conciliation attempts as counseling where a third party will be observing and offering suggestions or mediating conversation. Fears of being told that "Yes, he (she) is right - you are wrong here," can frighten away those who might ordinarily want to strive for re-connection.

This isn't the way that counselors and therapists work with couples. Their role is not to affix blame or judge the values and the actions of the couple, but to help them see their own alternatives more clearly, and to give them coaching where they need it to be able to talk in a way where both can learn and listen.

DON'T BE AFRAID to change your mind about something you've thought for a long time.

DON'T BE AFRAID to see things differently than you did before.

DON'T BE AFRAID to admit to yourself (and to your partner) that your partner has given you a new perspective on all or part of the situation.

DON'T BE AFRAID to admit that you are seeing things differently even as you are in the midst of talking about an issue.

DON'T BE AFRAID to have more positive feelings about your relationship.

DON'T BE AFRAID to understand and feel compassion for your partner.

DON'T BE AFRAID to be understood.

128

I COULDN'T ADMIT IT AT THE TIME, BUT. . .

Remember when you were arguing with your partner, in the midst of defending your position, when you suddenly saw things differently?

Remember when you were pretending to be "tough" when you actually felt scared and weak?

Remember when you were arguing about money, but thinking about how your feelings had been hurt the night before?

Remember?

FINISH THE FOLLOWING STATEMENTS AND SHARE YOUR RESPONSES WITH YOUR PARTNER.

I couldn't admit it at the time, but_____.

I couldn't admit it at the time, but_____.

I couldn't admit it at the time, but_____.

I couldn't admit it at the time, but_____.

I couldn't admit it at the time, but_____.

I couldn't admit it at the time, but_____.

I couldn't admit it at the time, but_____.

How do you feel when you say these things to your partner (or to yourself)
Is it embarrassing? Is it a relief?

**notes/thoughts/ideas
talk to. . .
ask about. . .**

129

IT'S NOT ALWAYS EASY TO LISTEN TO YOUR PARTNER WHEN YOU ARE CONFUSED OR ANGRY. NOR IS IT ALWAYS EASY TO SHARE YOUR FEELINGS ABOUT ISSUES THAT ARE UPSETTING TO YOU. BUT IT IS ALWAYS IMPORTANT TO TRY.

THIS IS HOW I REALLY FEEL

Do you ever suspect that you aren't quite in touch with your feelings? Have friends or family suggested that you're not fully aware of how you respond to different situations?

If you grew up in a family where no one talked about their feelings - where everything was action and thoughts or there was an absence of emotional expression - you may have difficulty even identifying your feelings at any particular time. This can also occur if you have had experiences where it seemed necessary to deny the actual feelings that you were trying to express. Denying feelings can come from being in an environment where other people are afraid to hear what you have to say. They may be so caught up with their own problems, they cannot be concerned with yours. Or they may not know what to say when you tell about your "inner" life. They may feel anxious about being asked to provide sympathy or advice upon hearing your story. If this negative or lukewarm response happens to us as children or as adults, it can confuse us as to what feelings are "all right" to have, throwing our sense of emotional balance into question.

notes/thoughts/ideas
talk to. . .
ask about. . .

"I have to tell you something. The other day when I said I wasn't upset about you going on another trip? Well, I was."

Sandy grew up in a family where everyone was "cheery" all of the time. She never saw her parents fight or argue, she was encouraged to overlook problems with her brothers and sisters, and no one ever talked about subjects that were upsetting to them. She viewed this situation as optimal for a child - a home where there was no disruption or conflict. All through her school years she felt sorry for her friends who came from families where emotions ran high and new issues were always being resolved. It all seemed like an enormous waste about time.

During college, Sandy became aware that, although she was happy on the surface, a lot of the joy and spontaneity that she saw in her friends was missing from her own life. She never felt

131

highs or lows or got angry, and everything affected her in pretty much the same way. The ability to ride right over upset feelings and disappointments had always seemed like a gift to Sandy. It helped her deal with a busy life and gave her an advantage in coping with new situations that would have been stressful to many others. But there were times when Sandy's friends described her as "cool" and "distant". They didn't agree that not getting upset was necessarily the best solution or that it showed personal strength.

Sandy had more of a chance to ponder this message when she got together with Bud. Many times during the course of their relationship Bud would ask her what she was feeling, and she just didn't have an answer. When her grandfather died, this issue came into dramatic relief. She went home for the funeral and saw that her family was doing "fine." But when she came back to school, she had no motivation to work or play. She felt estranged from Bud and her other friends and had to drag herself out of bed every morning. When Bud asked her what was going on, she couldn't say - she felt that she was viewing her life from a great distance.

Sandy had been practicing her whole life to take the edge off her feelings. She had been coached and convinced by her very nice family to disregard all emotions that might "rock the boat." By the time she was a young adult, she had built a life of limited opportunities for herself. She didn't know what feelings were available and wasn't sure what behavior or emotion was appropriate in any given situation. The inconsistency of having loved her grandfather and not being able to grieve when he died was obvious even to her. After his death, she began the task of learning to honor the full range of very natural emotions that she touched on everyday.

Feelings can also go underground because of anger and depression. These two connected emotional states insist on taking precedence over all others. If we stay angry long enough, without expressing it or dealing with the source of our anger, we can cover ourselves with a blanket of depression that wipes out our ability to be spontaneous and to project a wide range of feelings. Strangely enough, when this happens many people don't think of anger as the force within; they have a sense of dullness or detachment. Anger is often running the show inside, causing other emotions to take on minor supporting roles. People who go through professional counseling frequently find that as they discover pockets of anger that have never been given their due expression, their ability to "feel" all other emotions increases.

THE RANGE OF POSSIBLE HUMAN EMOTIONS IS ENORMOUS. OUR HERITAGE AS THINKING, EMOTIONAL BEINGS GIVES US THE ABILITY TO RESPOND IN WONDERFUL AND SUBTLE WAYS. SOMETIMES WE HAVE TO PRACTICE TO GET THESE FEELINGS TO RISE TO THE SURFACE AND COLOR OUR LIVES.

FEELINGS AND EMOTIONS

FILL OUT THE CHARTS ON THE FOLLOWING PAGES.
CHECK THE COLUMN THAT WOULD BEST DESCRIBE YOU.

feelings	often feel this way	sometimes feel this way	never feel this way
happy			
sad			
calm			
satisfied			
joyous			
enthusiastic			
melancholy			
inspired			
pleased			
quiet			
grateful			
hollow			
aggressive			
passionate			
stretched			

feelings	often feel this way	sometimes feel this way	never feel this way
sorrowful			
relaxed			
complacent			
serene			
ecstatic			
depressed			
gloomy			
glad			
dismal			
flat			
excited			
seductive			
empty			
immobilized			
tender			

133

notes/thoughts/ideas
talk to. . .
ask about. . .

feelings	often feel this way	sometimes feel this way	never feel this way
aching			
worried			
cross			
lonely			
cold			
alarmed			
shocked			
insecure			
nervous			
pressured			
doubtful			
feisty			
alive			
repulsed			
weary			
nauseated			
sluggish			
torn			
weak			
loving			

feelings	often feel this way	sometimes feel this way	never feel this way
crushed			
afflicted			
wrathful			
pathetic			
upset			
cautious			
horrified			
impatient			
dependent			
suspicious			
awed			
bored			
distant			
preoccupied			
jealous			
mixed-up			
envious			
humble			
appealing			
paralyzed			

134

feelings	often feel this way	sometimes feel this way	never feel this way
cheery			
carefree			
spirited			
in the dumps			
moody			
generous			
low			
discontented			
exhilarated			
jubilant			
disappointed			
sparkling			
useless			
worthless			
out of sorts			
hypocritical			
phoney			
terrified			
tragic			
angry			

feelings	often feel this way	sometimes feel this way	never feel this way
lighthearted			
optimistic			
vivacious			
sullen			
sulky			
hilarious			
jolly			
discouraged			
playful			
thrilled			
choked up			
shameful			
fraudulent			
ill at ease			
ashamed			
fearful			
frightened			
fidgety			
panicky			
ardent			

notes/thoughts/ideas
talk to. . .
ask about. . .

135

notes/thoughts/ideas
talk to. . .
ask about. . .

feelings	often feel this way	sometimes feel this way	never feel this way
resentful			
irritated			
enraged			
annoyed			
proud			
provoked			
infuriated			
sullen			
indignant			
pained			
zealous			
eager			
bitter			
tired			
keen			
confused			
stubborn			
heartbroken			

feelings	often feel this way	sometimes feel this way	never feel this way
avid			
anxious			
furious			
desirous			
inflamed			
isolated			
offended			
distressed			
irate			
hurt			
creative			
curious			
frustrated			
cruel			
concerned			
bewildered			
fuming			
despairing			

136

REFLECT ON THE FOLLOWING QUESTIONS
SHARE YOUR RESPONSES WITH YOUR PARTNER

1. Were you surprised by the range of "feelings" that were listed on the charts?

notes/thoughts/ideas
talk to. . .
ask about. . .

2. Do you use these "feeling" words to describe what is happening with you? If your partner used these words, would it help you understand more clearly what he or she was saying and thinking?

3. In your family, what was the "range" of emotion that people seemed to feel? Did your parents get really angry? Did you see people being quite sad? Was joy a word that you would use to describe any one or any situation in your family?

4. Does the possibility of using these words to describe more accurately what you're going through seem frightening in any way? Why?

5. Have you had a period of time in your life when you felt "flat" and disconnected from the people around you? What was happening to you at that stage of your life? When did it start? What changed? Do you still feel that way?

I DIDN'T TELL YOU THE TRUTH
BECAUSE. . .

When the time comes around and the accusation is "YOU LIED TO ME!," the <u>fact</u> that you didn't tell the truth is important to your partner. <u>Why</u> you didn't tell the truth is important to your relationship.

notes/thoughts/ideas
talk to. . .
ask about. . .

Kaye and Carlos were constantly fighting over who was telling the truth. More often than not, a two day argument would end up with one or the other "discovering" that their partner had been defending a "lie" all the time. These lies had to do with issues of spending time with friends and why they were late or hadn't kept their part of agreements. Kaye and Carlos were not just a couple who lied to each other, they were individuals with many fears about telling the truth. They had both come from families where the truth was "stretched". There were often extreme punishments and recriminations that followed any such revelation, so they learned early on to cover up their actions and innermost thoughts.

In order to have a healthy relationship Kaye and Carlos had to learn to trust each other with information about their lives and take responsibility for the ways in which they were trying to live. As adults, it became necessary for them to think in a long-range fashion before they acted, so they didn't have to cover their tracks with half-truths.

"You lied to me. . ."

They also had to learn to understand each other's fears about telling the truth and their bad habits of lying. Once they could "take the heat off" exposing feelings and vulnerabilities, they could both relax. This didn't happen overnight, but admitting the struggle that they were involved in was the first step and eventually led them to open-hearted communication.

The following list of phrases came from a half-hour conversation with a group of friends. These people were asked to spontaneously finish the statement, "I didn't tell you the truth because. . ." The activity itself was the stimulus for a lot of back and forth banter about relationships and truth-telling. It started a round of hours-long conversation about why people don't tell the truth, what their feelings are about being "exposed", what they do if they've been lied to, and all variations on this theme. This group's ability to bring to mind so many cliches around this issue points out how common this theme is for many individuals and couples.

DO ANY OF THESE SOUND FAMILIAR TO YOU?

I didn't tell you the truth because. . .

I was afraid of the consequences.

I didn't know how to say it.

I couldn't face up to the truth myself.

It was in my past and I thought it was irrelevant.

It was none of your business.

You'd never have let me forget it.

I was afraid I'd hurt you (I was afraid you'd hurt me).

I was telling you what you wanted to hear.

I thought you'd make more of it than it warranted.

What you don't know doesn't hurt you.

I thought you'd never trust me again.

Some things are better left unsaid.

I was waiting for the right time.

TRUTH AND FAMILY HISTORY

In some families, telling the truth at all costs is the law of the family. In other families, people hedge and color their experiences and stories of their lives. Telling the truth becomes more complex as you question whether or not you are "telling the truth" about how you <u>feel</u> rather than about what you have <u>done</u>. There is much to know about why you or others might have a tendency to "color the truth" in any particular situation.

notes/thoughts/ideas
talk to. . .
ask about. . .

1. **Do you remember a time in your parents' relationship when "telling the truth" made things better? What did you learn from that situation?**

2. **Do you remember a time when it made things worse? What did you learn from that situation?**

3. **What about in your own life - give an example of a time when you or someone close to you told the truth in a difficult situation and it made things better. What did you learn or conclude from that experience?**

4. **Give an example of a time in your own life when telling the truth in a difficult situation made things worse. What did you learn from that experience?**

5. **We can all think of an instance when "telling the truth" changed things forever. What is yours?**

MYTH NUMBER SIX
WORKING ON A RELATIONSHIP IS JUST THAT -
TOO MUCH WORK

Does working on a relationship seem just like that - a lot of "work"? Often one person in the partnership wants to (and does) "examine" the workings and observe the successes and failures of the time together. The other person may seem to have to be motivated to participate in the "work" of the relationship. This is a difficult situation as it highlights the differences in attitudes and values that make us individuals with individual styles of defining intimacy with loved ones.

1. Do you know a couple that spends an inordinate amount of time working out their conflicts? Would you describe this style as being too "analytical"? How has this couple influenced your ideas of how you want to "work things out"?

2. Do you know a couple that gets along very, very well and seems to have an easy time keeping it that way? Ask them to tell you some of their philosophies and ideas for achieving intimacy without beating a relationship into the ground.

3. Who are the models in your own family? Describe your father's approach. What was your mother's? Which of them are you like? Why? Does it work for you?

4. What are the "light" things that you do to be closer to your partner? Do you spend time alone, caring for each other? Do you go out and attend events that you both enjoy? Do you have inspiring friends? If not, why not?

143

CHAPTER SEVEN

SURVIVING

SEXUALITY
DIFFERENCES AND INDIFFERENCES

Questions and answers about sexuality are a common topic of conversation among everyone from children to the elderly. People of all ages wonder whether their own sexuality is "normal" or "usual" or "correct." Information to answer these questions is gleaned from films, books and eavesdropping on conversations heard everywhere. These most basic and primal issues on the planet - sexuality and reproduction - don't lose their impact just because we grow up and become educated or more conservative or more world-weary. Raising these topics always has the ability to make us snap to attention, and couples are particularly mindful of this part of human existence.

notes/thoughts/ideas
talk to. . .
ask about. . .

Finding comfort within ourselves regarding our sexual needs and desires is a goal of many individuals. It takes years of introspection and personal observation to come up with the answers that fit for you. When you add the hopes and dreams and confusions of another party, perhaps the person you have chosen to have a child with, there is ample room for renewed interest and reworking of issues that you thought were put to rest years before.

Of course, as you are learning through this book and by talking with others, becoming pregnant and having a child will add its own dimension of harmony or disharmony to your lives. And, as a couple, you will be unusual (and fortunate) if your sexual differences and indifferences do not give you cause for alarm during this critical period of life change - becoming parents.

Nora and Greg were new parents. They had been together for ten years as a couple - living together during college and then moving to the same city to begin their careers. Their sexual relationship had been fairly steady over the years; they made love two or three times a week. Neither of them had any real complaints about the other's responsiveness or caring in this department and didn't anticipate any changes once they had a child. Why would they? They already had a long-term history together. They felt that they knew each other very well.

During the first months of her pregnancy, Nora felt very sexual and was delighted to have physical attention from Greg. Her body seemed to be highly "tuned" and both Nora and Greg were excited by this bright aspect of their time together. They found it freeing not to worry about avoiding pregnancy and were reminded of some of their early romantic adventures back in college. As the months went on, however, Nora's body

147

started to feel very sensitive when it was touched. The feelings didn't seem to be sensual or even sexual, but rather "intrusive." While Greg was thrilled by her body as it changed shape, Nora felt depressed and self-conscious. As time went on, his attentions made her uneasy and she felt herself withdrawing emotionally as well as physically.

After Baby Janice was born, Greg was eager to resume their sexual relationship. He was well aware of the physical trauma of the birth (he had been an active participant, coaching Nora during labor and "catching" Janice as she was born), but he was also anxious to make love again. It had been several months since he and Nora had been sexually intimate. Nora expected to feel romantically inclined toward Greg after the birth, but was exhausted and fearful of being hurt. She read Greg's attempts at affection as pressuring her into having sex when she wasn't ready. She began to resent him for not understanding that she wasn't ready, and not recognizing the stress her body had been through.

For Nora and Greg, much of what she communicated was that she was starting to feel depressed and anxious about her lack of sexuality. Although she didn't want to be "pressured" by Greg to make love, she was also acutely aware of the fact that never before would she have used the term "pressure" to define his affection and attention. Greg, for his part, was doubting Nora's attraction to him as a partner. He was feeling rejected on a daily basis, not only as a lover, but as a friend - he was getting the message that he was making her feel worse every time he wanted to discuss his feelings. He began to think that it wasn't okay for him to have his desires for Nora - that he was being a bully and inconsiderate.

At one point, Nora suggested to Greg that he find someone else to sleep with, if his desires were so strong and he was so upset by her lack of response. For Greg, this was a devastating suggestion that left him feeling detached from Nora and confused about the direction of their relationship. Nora, on the other hand, made this statement out of fear and longing and anxiety. She didn't really want Greg to find someone else, but she was beginning to feel tremendously guilty for not wanting to be a sexual partner.

"Can you tell me more about how you feel? I want to help. Does it have to do with something I said or did?"

One day she sat down with Greg and explained her feelings by calling to mind a car accident Greg had been in four years before. She asked Greg how he would have felt if she had been coaxing him to walk sooner than he felt able. How would he have reacted if she had been angry because he couldn't go jogging with her when his leg and hip were in a full cast. How would he have responded if she had insisted on his taking long drives in the car while he was still feeling fragile and vulnerable?

The analogy was extreme, but it was the beginning of renewed communication. It gave Greg a starting point for really understanding Nora's feelings and allowed Nora to establish a frame of reference that made sense to her and eased her guilt feelings about her reactions since the birth. Nora and Greg were lucky. They found a way to break through their communication barrier before they became totally alienated. Not every couple is so adept at finding analogies that work so well. But because issues of sexuality are so integral in the experience of pregnancy and birth, it is essential that each couple become very creative to get information about feelings and fears across to their partner.

Now we can also ask, what would have happened if Nora and Greg were caught not just in the midst of miscommunication and hurt feelings over their waning sexuality, but were actually experiencing some of the fallout from Postpartum Depression? What if Nora was experiencing the very common depletion in hormones that carry with them a lack of interest in sex after the birth of a child? What kind of struggles might they have had if they were attempting to understand the changes in their sexual relationship, trying day after day to figure out why Nora's feelings had changed and were not coming up with any answers? Is it possible that having the knowledge that this is a common phenomenon would have provided relief and comfort during the time of transition?

For all couples who experience changes in their sexual relationship after having a baby, it is essential to consider the possibility that physiological changes are creating a reduction in sexual drive, and that there is every reason to believe that sexual urges and interest will resurface at the pre-pregnancy level, although maybe not for many months. This type of understanding can alleviate the bitterness and fears that often go unchecked when couples who are misinformed (or uninformed) about the true nature of postpartum physiology blame each other and their relationship for the sexual changes that occur.

QUESTIONS AND ANXIETIES ABOUT SEXUALITY CAN COLOR ALL PARTS OF A COUPLE RELATIONSHIP. FURTHERMORE, THESE THOUGHTS AND CONCERNS CAN SERIOUSLY AFFECT YOUR OWN SELF-PERCEPTIONS AND SELF-ESTEEM.

REFLECTING ON NORA AND GREG'S STORY

What parts of Nora and Greg's story sound familiar to you? What aspects or feelings are similar to your own?

What would you have said to help this couple by either offering information or reassurance?

1.

2.

3.

What else do you think tbey needed to say to each other?

1.

2.

3.

YOUR OWN FEELINGS ABOUT SEXUALITY

Are <u>you</u> comfortable talking with <u>your</u> partner about your sexual desires or fears or concerns? If not, why not?

Have you ever had a sexual partner who made you feel uncomfortable about talking about sex? If you have a negative feeling from the past, is it still appropriate today, or is it a "left-over" fear?

Do you find this topic stressful? Why? What time in your life does it remind you of? Who does it remind you of? How are you different now?

What can your partner do or say to "set the stage" and make communication happen more easily? Have you told him or her? If not, why not?

1.

2.

3.

SHARE THESE THOUGHTS AND FEELINGS WITH YOUR PARTNER

PHASES OF SEXUALITY

notes/thoughts/ideas
talk to. . .
ask about. . .

FILL OUT THE FOLLOWING TIME LINE.
Mark the areas on the time line when you felt sexually "confident" or "happy" or
"scared" or "insecure". (e.g. at 17, I felt very scared; at 22, I felt very desirable and secure)

_____

10 yrs   15 yrs   20 yrs   25 yrs   30 yrs   35 yrs   40 yrs   45 yrs   50 yrs   55 yrs

IDENTIFY THE HIGHPOINTS AND THE LOWPOINTS OF YOUR TIME LIME.

What was happening in your education or career at each point?

What was happening in your family life?

How old were you?

How was your physical health?
        poor _____ fair _____ good _____ excellent _____

How would you describe your mental/emotional health?

        poor _____ fair _____ good _____ excellent _____

152

How do <u>you</u> define sexually "confident" or "happy?" What does that statement mean to <u>you</u>?

<u>What</u> does it remind you of?

<u>Who</u> does it remind you of? Is that person still in your life now?

<u>How</u> are you different now?

How do you define sexually "scared" or "insecure?" What does that statement mean to you?

<u>What</u> does it remind you of?

<u>Who</u> does it remind you of?

<u>How</u> are you different now?

153

Did your sexuality at these high and low points affect your self-concept in other areas of your life? How?

Did your self-concept during these times affect your sexuality? How?

Would you describe yourself as a person with sexual phases or cycles? To what do they seem to be connected in your life? Is this something you've thought about before?

Does the thought of having sexual phases or cycles seem stressful or relaxing? Why?

From thinking about these questions what are you learning about yourself that you didn't know before?

154

SEXUALITY AND YOUR PARENTS

Sex and your parents - what do those words have to do with each other anyway? So many people know so little about how their parents loved and made love that it is common to hear jokes like, "Well, I know they did it at least three times - I've got a brother and a sister!"

If you don't know how your parents acted or felt when it came to sex, then you're missing an important model in your life that could provide valuable clues for how you would like to (or not like to) act yourself.   If you're missing this model, then you must create your own - from your heart, your intuition, your "sense" of what is right for you, and from listening to the people around you who have developed their own workable (or not so workable) approaches to love and sex.

If you do know how your parents felt and acted, then you should spend a little time organizing that information to draw some conclusions that reflect your own attitudes and behaviors. Those parents who gave out definite messages about this important area of life will have made an imprint that is hard to ignore.   Understanding this imprint is a key to resolving your own life experience.

What do you know about your parents' sexual experiences over the years? Did they make love on the first date? The tenth date? Did they wait until they were married? How do you know these things?

How did your parents religious and cultural backgrounds influence their views on sexuality? Did they come from the same backgrounds? If not, how were they different? Which of these messages did they pass on to you?

Are your parents physically affectionate without being sexual? Was this a common part of the family experience - to see your parents showing physical affection?

155

Is it easy or difficult for you to see your parents as sexual beings? Now that <u>you</u> are a parent, do you see yourself in the same way that you viewed your parents?

Do you remember your parents speaking openly about their sexuality? Do you think they spoke about their desires and concerns in private?

MESSAGES FROM PARENTS ABOUT SEXUALITY

What were the main messages that your <u>mother</u> passed on to you about sexuality?

You should _____

You should never _____

When it comes to sex, women _____

When it comes to sex, men _____

Conversations about sex are _____

What were the main messages that your <u>father</u> passed on to you about sexuality?

You should _____

You should never _____

When it comes to sex, women _____

When it comes to sex, men _____

Conversations about sex are _____

156

SEX AND PREGNANCY

SURVEYING FRIENDS AND NEIGHBORS

Start a conversation about sex and pregnancy with parents you know (what about your own?). What do they have to say?

notes/thoughts/ideas
talk to. . .
ask about. . .

Ask five couples who have children if, and how, their sex lives changed after pregnancy and childbirth. If possible, ask them when they are together.

How many felt it changed for the better? _____ for the worse? _____

How many partners had different perceptions about the changes? _____

How many expressed feelings of anxiety over the changes? _____

How many said they expected it to change? _____

How many feel comfortable with their sex lives now? _____

How long did it take for them to establish a new (or satisfying) post-pregnancy routine? _____

How many connected a change in feelings of sexuality with physiological (bodily) changes that accompanied pregnancy? _____

What suggestions or advice or reassuring statements did you hear from these people?

1.

2.

3.

157

What is the most valuable information or insight that you didn't know (hadn't thought of) before that you learned from talking to these couples?

If you were being surveyed by another couple, how would you answer the same questions?

What would be your advice, suggestions or reassurances for others?

1.

2.

3.

4.

5.

**SPEND SOME TIME TALKING WITH YOUR PARTNER
ABOUT THE COUPLES YOU SURVEYED AND WHAT YOU LEARNED**

MONEY

Money - how you get it and what you do with it is an ever-present issue in this society. People argue about not having enough money, dad or mom working too hard to get the money that's coming in, the other partner not working hard enough, what to do about the kids' allowances, whether or not to save for college. . . the list goes on and on. Money can be the real issue, or it can be the surface issue that other, deeper problems hide behind.

Depending on your family history, your personal experiences over many years, your age and your sex, money may be a "loaded" issue for you, or not concern you at all. In an age where more and more women are entering the workforce, and contributing heftily (if not totally) to the couple finances, traditional roles of who makes the money, who spends it, and who gets to make the financial decisions are overthrown. Men and women must be aware of the struggles that couples go through to achieve "equity" in both earning and spending.

Familial and societal expectations about money get passed down through the generations. Though many couples today struggle to establish a groundwork of equality where money is concerned, they may still be grappling with the same kinds of money issues that disturbed their parents and grandparents years ago.

Thomas and Susan were the "model couple" for others in their social group. Sure, they had disagreements about issues, mostly centering around their very different attitudes toward saving and spending money, but they were always able to sit down and come to an amicable compromise. For five years of courtship and marriage, they prided themselves on their ability to work together to solve conflicts. In fact, they often acted as a sounding board for friends who didn't have a clue about where to start to settle arguments!

Thomas and Susan were in for a shock. After the birth of their first child, they found that disagreements were often left hanging from day to day. The ways they had talked about

"With daycare and all, I don't think I can earn enough to make a job worth my while. Should I be working or staying at home?"

things in the past just didn't seem to be working for them now. On many occasions, a discussion would end with Susan crying and Thomas storming out of the house - two types of behavior that were never seen during their courting and early years of marriage.

They both felt on edge - every day they were determined to handle arguments in a more relaxed manner, but this resolve only lasted for a matter of hours. They were upset over the new stresses in their life as parents, and even more, they feared what it would mean for them as a couple and a new family if they didn't calm down and get their life together without yelling and screaming.

Thomas was suddenly horrified at Susan's spending patterns. "You scare me with that lackadaisical approach. You've gotten pretty foolhardy with the money, and now we only have one salary to depend on!" Susan's retort that she wasn't spending any more than she did before the baby was born did not convince Thomas - he was anxious about the finances and the exact dollar figures weren't really the problem.

"Now that I have a baby, I get terrified thinking about house and car payments, what to do for insurance. . ."

Deep inside Susan felt it was okay for Thomas to be concerned about the money but that he was too anxious and was making her feel guilty about every expenditure. "I feel choked if I can't buy what I want for my own home, and make my own baby comfortable. I've worked for years to get to this point, and I don't want someone else telling me what to do with every penny, just because now I'm at home with a child!" Her family history played a big part, too, as she described her growing up years: "My mother always bought anything she wanted for the house and my father was thrilled! He wasn't a penny-pincher, and my mother never worked outside the home a day in her life!"

The rules can change just when you think you have them well-understood. Changes in income (because of a windfall or a downfall) can easily upset the income applecart. Changing the status of the couple by marriage (or separation) can add another dimension, and the dramatic emotional and financial shift that many people go through after they have a child must also be taken into account. Each of these life events brings with it the seeds that were planted by parents and experiences long ago. Many of these seeds are the rules and assumptions that have to do with keeping individuals and families financially solvent. If you don't understand how they are affecting you, you will be missing a big key as to why you are making some of your most basic life decisions today.

FEARS ABOUT MONEY

For some people, the "fears" they have about money run so deep that they overshadow all desires and rational ways of looking at finances.

Peter was a happy-go-lucky young man, until it came to money. When he went out with friends, he wanted to be generous and pay for meals, or buy people spontaneous gifts, but his fears about not having enough money wouldn't let him do those things. He felt guilty about his reluctance to spend and was afraid others saw him as a stingy person.

He hated that part of himself, but would get so nervous when the check came, that he sometimes broke out in a cold sweat. What about? He feared that he wouldn't have enough money with him (he always did) or that the check wouldn't be divided up correctly and he would end up paying more than his share. Even with people he dearly loved, he found it hard to break down this anxiety.

One might think that Peter came from a very poor family where it was necessary to watch every penny. Strangely enough, this wasn't so. Peter's family was typically middle class with both parents working - never a lot of extra money to go around, but enough that the family didn't have to worry. So the problem wasn't the financial situation of his immediate family, but rather the fact that both of his parents had lived through the Depression and were careful about what they spent and where they spent it. Peter heard many stories about his parents' and grandparents' struggles during the Depression years, and even though it had happened before he was born, the message came through loud and clear - careful spending and saving are values to hang on to.

WHAT ARE <u>YOUR</u> FEARS AND INSECURITIES ABOUT MONEY?

1. When it comes to money, I'm afraid _____

2. I get nervous when I have to spend money on _____

3. I don't like the way I handle money when _____

4. The worst time of my life in regard to money was _____

5. The last thing I'd spend extra money on is _____

161

WHAT IS <u>YOUR</u> FAMILY STORY IN RELATION TO MONEY AND WHAT TO SPEND IT ON?

notes/thoughts/ideas
talk to. . .
ask about. . .

1. What were the family priorities? Who made the spending decisions?

2. What part did your mother play? Describe her attitude about money.

3. What part did your father play? Describe his attitude about money.

4. Were the children in the family allowed to "vote" on spending decisions?

5. Did decisions about spending money happen easily or with difficulty?

6. How is your present attitude reminiscent of your parents'? How is it different? Have these been conscious decisions?

CONCERNS OVER MONEY - HOW IT IS MADE AND HOW IT IS SPENT - ARE EPIDEMIC IN OUR SOCIETY. IT IS ESSENTIAL TO UNDERSTAND YOUR OWN PERSONAL "MONEY DYNAMICS" AND HISTORY AND THAT OF YOUR PARTNER. FROM THIS SHARING YOU CAN DEVELOP A PLAN THAT WILL ADDRESS BOTH OF YOUR NEEDS AND CONCERNS.

FINANCIAL DEPENDENCE AND INDEPENDENCE

Am I leaning too hard on my partner financially or not hard enough? This is a question that many men and women grapple with as they try a financial balancing act in a committed relationship. There are many questions to ask about this issue:

notes/thoughts/ideas
talk to. . .
ask about. . .

When both people work, should the income be shared or kept separate?   What about when there is an obvious disparity in the amount of income earned?

Jeanne and Charles prided themselves on keeping their money separate. They had dated for several years before they married and had a child, and during that period of time, they each paid their own way. When they dated they lived in separate apartments and paid for vacations, nights out, etc. from their own funds. If one of them didn't have enough money, the other person would sometimes pick up the tab, but this was rare. They felt very mature about their "enlightened" stance, even as they carried it with them into marriage and parenthood.

Once they married, Charles' income took a leap forward (he also had some "family money" to draw on) , but Jeanne's stayed basically the same. They kept the same arrangements about money, each paying half the house payment, half the food, and keeping finances separate but equal. The problem became obvious very quickly, however, as Charles resented the fact that Jeanne could not afford to "play" at the same level as he, and was not interested in spending money on many things that would have indicated their "upward" mobility. She was struggling to make ends meet (and cover her obligations), but had no money left over for frivolities.

The financial partnership that had worked so well before having a child now seemed ludicrous to their friends. How were these people going to live with a marriage and a child if Jeanne couldn't be part of Charles' success and was constantly scrambling to keep her head above water - trying to live according to Charles' standard of living?

EACH PARTNERSHIP WILL MAKE ITS OWN UNIQUE ARRANGEMENTS, BUT THAT WON'T HAPPEN COMFORTABLY UNLESS EACH PERSON KNOWS WHAT HIS OR HER LIMITS ARE. THE SET OF "RULES" THAT WORKED BEFORE A MARRIAGE DO NOT ALWAYS WORK AFTER, AND TEND TO CHANGE AGAIN WHEN A CHILD IS BORN.

163

SPENDING MONEY - YOUR PRIORITIES

FILL OUT THE FOLLOWING CHART.

Use numbers 1 to 5 to indicate the importance of the items to you, with 1 being the most important and 5 being the least important.

	Rating	Comments
Your own education		
Children's education		
Saving money		
Nice clothing		
Toys for birthdays, holidays		
Educational toys		
Own property/Own house		
Have a new car		
Go on vacations		
Eat out		
Take care of parents		

SHARE YOUR RESPONSES WITH YOUR PARTNER

FINANCIAL ARRANGEMENTS

FILL OUT THE FOLLOWING CHART.
SHARE YOUR RESPONSES WITH YOUR PARTNER

notes/thoughts/ideas
talk to. . .
ask about. . .

Our financial arrangements:

While we were dating	After we got married	Now that we have a child

Were these joint agreements? _____ Yes _____ No

Did you actually work them out, or did they just fall into place?_____.

How do you feel about the current status? _____.

What are the problems with the current arrangement?

    1.

    2.

    3.

What are the advantages of the current arrangement?

    1.

    2.

    3.

WHAT SHOULD WE SPEND THE MONEY ON?

notes/thoughts/ideas
talk to. . .
ask about. . .

Once you've <u>got</u> the income, then you have to decide what you're going to spend it on. For some couples this is easy, for others it's pure torture.

Mike told the following story about the way financial decisions were made when he was growing up: In his family everything was divided into short-term versus long-term funds. Short-term money was set aside for entertainment and temporary items like clothing and toys. Long-term money was put into a special account for education and vacations and buying a home. His parents put their emphasis on the long-term goals. They saved for the "bigger" things in life and skipped the smaller day-to-day purchases.

In Mike's cousin's family, his aunt and uncle gave his cousin everything he wanted, but when the time came for him to go to college, no one had made any provisions, and he couldn't go until he had worked for several years to save the money. As Mike remembers, "Of all of the cousins, Jim had the most possessions and we were all jealous, but after high school he couldn't go to college; we were set and he wasn't." That perception has formed Mike's ideas about how he will deal with his family finances.

"Don't you understand how I feel? In my family we <u>never</u> spent money on frivolous things like vacations."

Think of three couples you know who have successful relationships - how do they handle their financial decisions and share (or not share) their finances?   What have you learned from them? What do they do that can be applied to <u>your</u> financial partnership?

FATIGUE

Fatigue, exhaustion and general tiredness can be a source of great concern and conflict in a partnership after the birth of a baby or during other times of stress in your life. How big an issue is fatigue in your life? For some women, having a baby brings a reservoir of health and energy to the surface. It provides a super charge of well-being that makes them feel more productive and "alive" than ever before. For a greater number of women, however, having a baby brings exhaustion that is both unexpected and strangely depleting. They expect to be brimming with energy, but find they can hardly stay awake past 7:30 PM, even with a two-hour nap during the day. There are many reasons for this phenomenon. Some or all may be affecting any individual new mother, and some concern fathers who are also caregivers.

1-**Taking care of a child on a twenty-four hour-a-day maintenance schedule means that you are never really "off-duty."** Even if the actual care demands don't seem to be that great, what other jobs do you know of that require this kind of attention? How long do you think you'd last if your boss at work demanded that you be available twenty-four hours a day for several years, with possibly no extra financial rewards? (Don't worry, your room and board and other expenses would be covered). Does it sound like a job that you'd be signing up for? How much stress would it add to your workday if you were the person responsible for finding your replacement every time you were ill or wanted to take a day off or needed to run a few errands? Sound tiring to you? It is, and of course the job is known as being a full-time parent.

"I never knew I could be so tired! I can hardly hold my head up to read this book."

2 - **The hormonal and physiological changes that pregnant women and new mothers experience are often accompanied by exhaustion.** During pregnancy a woman's body is creating a new life that must grow to viable size and strength - all in the remarkably short time of nine months. This is a big job no matter what the time frame that is allotted, so women naturally tend to "gear down" during this phase and center their concentration on this complex inner process of creating a new human being. In the first three months of pregnancy, a woman may literally need to sleep eighteen or twenty hours a day. Unfortunately, our society doesn't have a lot of fine-tuned words to account for this type of natural behavior, so both men and women may have concerns about what this really "means." They may wonder if everything is okay, if the woman is upset

167

about the pregnancy, or unhappy with the relationship. Studies show that after birthing, many women have a lowered level of thyroid in the system. Even for people who are not postpartum, this state is usually accompanied by fatigue. Ordinarily the individual would be treated by a physician who is concerned about the woman's "tiredness," does a physical to determine whether or not she has a hypothyroid condition and then prescribes medication which will boost the level of thyroid in the body and alleviate the symptoms. <u>For women who are postpartum, however, this type of physical evaluation rarely occurs, and they are left to deal with the consequences of a very real depletion of essentials hormone in the body.</u>

3 - **Depression is a state of emotional and often physical withdrawal that can be accompanied by extreme sleepiness or exhaustion.** Depression may signal feelings of isolation or helplessness and it may indicate that the new parent is feeling "overwhelmed" by this new role and hasn't had time to adjust. Hormonal changes can create the symptomatology of depression as well. Once again, "the medical experts in the field of Postpartum Depression say that a diminished level of thyroid in the system can be the culprit and that many women experience relief if put on a medication schedule that boosts this hormone level in the bloodstream. Because this has been a neglected field of study for so long, it is highly likely that women who have this concern and are interested in

"We did pretty good last night. We got at least three hours sleep. Uh oh. I hear the baby. I'll be right back."

pursuing this line of help will have to educate their physicians as to the possibilities of the association between depression, exhaustion, and postpartum hormonal levels.

4 - **Having a baby is the equivalent of having major surgery.** The effect on a woman's body is intense and traumatic. Despite the fact that giving birth is obviously a common experience, it still is a tremendous stressor to a woman's physical and psychological being. The recovery time goes beyond the days that immediately follow the birth. The body must wind down from the pregnancy, the

birth, the recovery, and then adjust to the new role of motherhood. Part of the adjustment of going through these phases may include feeling very tired. We all know these events must happen, but we don't always take seriously just how they will affect us, and how long it may take to return to "normal."

5 - Babies who don't sleep through the night do something very obvious to their parents (especially the parents who get up to see what is wrong) - they interrupt their sleep cycle. For parents whose new babies are having a difficult time adjusting to the world, a "good night's sleep" may be a distant memory. It might not be so bad if you didn't have to get up in the morning and live the rest of your life, doing errands and carrying on daily tasks, but most of us do. So, we go to these daily jobs with a minimum of energy and we feel tired.

6 - Babies who cry a lot, either at night or during the day, are also adding to the general level of exhaustion that parents feel. It is not easy to hear a baby cry (even if you aren't the parent) without feeling some of the baby's stress yourself. Constant anxiety and stress are common percursors to fatigue. So, crying from your newborn may feel like a strain on your mental state, but it is also wearing down your physical ability to combat exhaustion.

7 - Nursing a baby can also be tiring. Your baby is literally living off of your body, and demanding more nourishment all the time. Your body must take in and produce enough food for two people - and this is quite an expectation (although quite a natural one, of course). Even though it is natural, it doesn't diminish the fact that it is adding another great source of fatigue to your system. Even after you stop nursing, it usually takes several months to regain your "pre-pregnancy" level of energy.

8 - A common response to new situations and new life roles is to become tired. Travelers and students and men and women going through a personal crisis may all wish to sleep through the transition. Through fatigue, new parents may be expressing a need to slide into the role of parenthood and guardianship slowly, rather than having it thrust upon them. They may be recovering their strength in many ways, and sleeping may speed this process along.

You can certainly think of even more reasons for fatigue in a new mother and new father. In this culture, there is a certain air of dismissal for those who are "tired too much;" this complaint isn't taken too seriously. This societal attitude adds to whatever other feelings new parents may have, increasing tension in the home. The mother may feel guilty for not being as energetic as she was before she had the baby. The new father may feel resentful that his efforts to keep work and home and personal life together are not recognized as equally taxing.

169

THE ENERGY GRAPH

FILL IN THE GRAPH SHOWING YOUR "ENERGY" LEVELS OVER YOUR LIFETIME.

LABEL THE HIGHS AND LOWS.

What was happening in your life at those times? Physically? Emotionally? Career-wise? Education-wise? With relationships? What do you expect to see on the graph in the coming years?

SHARE THIS INFORMATION WITH YOUR PARTNER.

NOT GETTING ENOUGH REST AS NEW PARENTS CAN PUT A TREMENDOUS STRAIN ON THE COUPLE RELATIONSHIP. IT BEHOOVES NEW PARENTS TO DO EVERYTHING THEY CAN TO HELP EACH OTHER FIND SOLUTIONS FOR BRINGING MORE ENERGY BACK INTO THEIR LIVES.

170

PREGNANCY, NEW PARENTHOOD AND FATIGUE

1. Now that you are a parent, what role does "being tired" play in your life and your couple relationship?

notes/thoughts/ideas
talk to. . .
ask about. . .

2. What feelings do you have about being tired? Is it okay with you? Is it depressing? Do you feel guilty about being tired? If so, where did that feeling originate?

3. Have you changed your expectations of what you can get done during the day to accomodate this new role of being a parent? How? Does your partner agree?

   I used to be able to _____, now I can _____.

   I used to be able to _____, now I can _____.

   I used to be able to _____, now I can _____.

   I used to be able to _____, now I can _____.

4. If you are tired, do you ask for assistance from others with childcare responsibilities as well as other daily tasks? If not, why not?

171

5. Do both you and your partner feel the same about having "extended family" members (e.g. neighbors, sisters, brothers, cousins) help relieve the burden of new activities and child care? If not, describe how you each see this issue.

6. "Being tired" is a common theme with new parents. Do you know parents who have had conflicts over this issue? If so, what were their understandings and/or solutions?

1.

2.

3.

4.

5.

IT IS OFTEN NECESSARY TO CALL ON FRIENDS AND NEIGHBORS FOR HELP GETTING THROUGH THIS TIME OF TRANSITION. IT IS AN ARENA WHERE OTHER PEOPLE CAN, AND DO, MAKE THE DIFFERENCE THROUGH THEIR HELP WITH CHILD CARE AND SOLUTIONS TO NEW PARENT DILEMMAS. IF YOU'VE GOT IDEAS, PASS THEM ON!

MOODS AND DEPRESSION

In my heart, I am sure that a major task of human beings is to understand the depth of despair that our loved ones may feel. This is an especially potent concern when it comes to couple relationships and keeping families together.

Experiencing "depression" is different from being "upset" or "bummed out" or "down." We all have our days when nothing goes right, when we wish we hadn't gotten out of bed, when gloom or pessimism pervades our hours. To be "out of sorts" is to experience the opposite of feeling joy or happiness, but it is usually a term reserved for a temporary condition. It is a different state of mind from the deep-seated, all pervasive sense of flatness and detachment that is often called "depression."

Depression is despair. It speaks of hopelessness and fear of never feeling happy again. It seems to defeat all efforts to be cleared up or overcome. Life has taken on a quality that fights obvious assistance. Solutions which are obvious to others are not acted upon, there seems to be no energy to move on from this quagmire. But, that's why they call it depression - it is. And it isn't easy.

People of all ages can feel depression. Young children, teenagers, those in mid-life and the elderly are all susceptible. Depressed feelings can be precipitated by a trauma, by another's life crisis, by hormonal changes. For some it seems to come from "nowhere." If you have never felt such depression yourself, you may nevertheless have been affected by it, as the chances are great that someone dear to you will struggle with this emotional distress. Many times it won't be until the crisis is over that you will know the extent of the difficulty that the individual was experiencing -what they were feeling and how it was affecting their lives.

The rather common societal problem of low-grade depression is not very clearly understood either by the millions of people who experience it, or the millions of mates, friends and relatives who observe it and are concerned about the change in feelings and behavior. Can others understand what to say or do, especially if they haven't been through such a time themselves? From those who are not experiencing this emotional crisis, you sometimes hear a refrain that goes, "Oh, he likes to be depressed. If he didn't, he'd do something about it." This statement tells us information about the speaker who is getting worn out with their friend's or relative's emotional down-time. It also signals a lack of understanding. People don't stay depressed because they "like" it. In fact, they are struggling hard to find solutions to bring their daily lives back into focus - but depression isn't an easy state of mind to triumph over.

173

Dismissing depression as an attention-getting device is a peculiar reaction to someone in a very difficult time of transition that happens to many people. Consider it this way - if someone is "trying to get attention" by being depressed, and that is the only way they can think of to draw attention to their plight, then don't we want to notice and offer assistance any way we can? We may not want to serve full-time as an active ear, but such pleas for help come from desperation and should not be belittled.

Depression can, and should, be understood from many perspectives. Symptoms may be similar in a variety of situations, but the causes may be quite different. For example, did you know that depression can be associated with

* many medicines prescribed by physicians, dentists and other health-care professionals
* hormonal changes during adolescence, pregnancy or mid-life
* recovery from surgery
* a major life crisis, such as the death of a loved one
* an international incident or natural disaster that does not directly touch anyone you know
* guilt over things said, or never said, things done or never done
* suppressed anger

To make matters worse, for some folks feeling depressed can cause deeper depression. Their sense of loss of control and unhappiness can seriously escalate fears of continued despair. Men and women may demonstrate this "depression" by having a loss of sexual interest, fatigue, listlessness, sleepiness, flatness of feelings or a sense of detachment from others.

After a time, an individual in the throes of depression may be deserted by friends or family who have tried to provide loving support during this difficult period of time. These people may give up despite their concerns and desire to help. They may feel that their support hasn't been graciously received, that their advice hasn't been acted upon, even that they are helping to perpetuate the person's despair by continuing to listen. As a concerned friend or partner, your words of encouragement are essential, but perhaps the best step is to help the friend who has "been there too long" to seek counseling from a minister, professional therapist, physician or other qualified person.

MANY MEN AND WOMEN HAVE FOUND RELIEF AND HOPE FROM HEARING THE VERY REAL STORIES OF OTHERS WHO HAVE MOVED PAST THIS TIME OF EMOTIONAL CHALLENGE AND ARE ON THE OTHER SIDE. IF YOU HAVE A STORY OF PROMISE, SHARE IT WITH SOMEONE YOU KNOW

PREGNANCY AND DEPRESSION

Although depression may be part of many lives, our focus here is on its role in the lives of new parents. Stories of depression and pregnancy/birthing are everywhere. "If I really want to have this child, why am I so depressed?" is a familiar query from both sexes. While both men and women have many new issues to examine and understand as parents, depression can tip the balance and make normal adjustments to parenting and coupling seem quite impossible. <u>Although the term "depression" covers many bases, it is quite important to separate out that depression which has to do with changes and stresses in life situations, and that which is the result of the post-birth physiology of the new mother.</u>

notes/thoughts/ideas
talk to. . .
ask about. . .

Throughout this manual, there are references to this Postpartum Depression. The reason is that this time of emotional stress pervades every area of the new family's life. It appears as exhaustion, confusion over sexuality, judgements about whether or not the new mother is trying hard enough to "recover" from the pregnancy and birth, anger, exacerbates sibling rivalries and sometimes even family violence. Because it is so little understood, the symptoms are often miscommunicated, misread and misinterpreted.

When we talk about postpartum physiology, we are not talking about weight gain, or loss of muscle tone or lusterless hair or any of the myriad of other "physical appearance" concerns that can happen in the nine month period and be disconcerting. Here we are talking about the very real physiological changes that are occurring internally and have to do with rapidly changing hormone levels. Dropping levels of thyroid and progesterone alone can explain both depression and fatigue in new mothers. And, the body is actually

"I know dear, it's okay to cry. Lots of women feel depressed after they have a baby. I know you feel discouraged, but it is normal and it may take awhile to get back on an even keel."

shifting large doses of many other hormones at the same time - some are starting up to encourage the production of breast milk, others are falling off since their job to prepare the body for pregnancy and birth is finished. **No matter what the combination, it is very important to realize that this massive alteration in body chemicals is more than enough to precipitate many types of emotional distress, even if the new mother is very competent, and very well-prepared for the role of parenting and has gone into the experience with nothing but joy and high expectations.**

POSTPARTUM DEPRESSION IS A COMPLICATED ISSUE FOR NEW PARENTS

Frequently, men and women do not want to discuss what is happening to them emotionally during pregnancy and after the birth because they feel shame or guilt. They may assume that having any "negative" feelings means that they are unhappy with the child or the couple relationship. They may feel confused about what the emotions actually mean, or feel isolated in their experience. I have heard women talk about depression during pregnancy, their fear of what they were thinking and feeling, yet say they never talked to a soul about it, including the doctor they were visiting on a regular basis for check-ups. Physicians have echoed this scenario - they have told me that they frequently get no news about the woman's fragile emotional state until they hear about it from someone else. This tendency of women to hold the fears inside may indicate that women who are going through this time of emotional struggle may not have any idea where to turn for relief. Is it appropriate to go to the obstetrician with talk about "baby blues" or should it be a psychiatrist or should it be the family doctor or should it be your best friend? Who amongst those who might ordinarily be seen as resources is the right person to give you aid when the subject is Postpartum Depression?

"I can remember the exact minute when I started to feel 'different.' We were on a plane going on vacation and I was one month pregnant. All of a sudden, I felt as if a large grey bird landed above me and spread its wings around me. It felt like I had withdrawn behind a thick grey veil. The feeling stayed with me throughout my pregnancy, and for about a year afterwards.

"At first I had the sense that I was just using my resources for the child that was growing inside. I wasn't very interested in my friends and didn't want to go anywhere. I worked during that period of time, but it was work by myself. I was exhausted for the first three months and my sexual interest almost completely disappeared. What had been an exciting and intimate sexual relationship with my husband turned overnight into a time that I can best describe as 'asexual.'

"I felt okay about all of this in the beginning, but after a while my husband started to question what my real feelings were for him. He began to lose faith that this really had to do with the pregnancy ('Did I still love him? Was there someone else? Didn't I find him attractive anymore?'). I guess I felt some of those same concerns, too. I kept wondering if sleeping all of the time, having no sexual interest and being alone might be the 'new me.' I think that was when I started to get scared and question our relationship and my own state of mind.

For a year I didn't think of it as 'depression,' but afterwards I started talking to women about their experiences during pregnancy and after childbirth and I attached the label "depression" to what I had been going through. It was a relief to have a word that categorized what I had been feeling. I also knew at that point that I certainly wasn't alone - it hadn't just been me and my inability to deal with things - it was a pretty common experience for a lot of people. I wish I'd known that at the time. And I wish my partner had known - it would have saved us a lot of pain."

In past years, it was not uncommon for women to be institutionalized after the birth of a child for what was called "Postpartum Psychosis or Depression." Although this is not always the answer to relieve the family's distress, hospitalization can be the answer for the woman who is frightened of "losing her mind," or hurting herself or her child or is feeling unable to cope with the demands of the new child due to emotional stress. It is a protective measure that allows physicians and mental health professionals to step in and use their expertise to get the woman and her family past the time of crisis. In England, the hospitalization of a woman experiencing postpartum psychosis and depression symptoms is considered to be a primary solution that can bring the family past the transition stage and entire hospitals are used just to care for the woman with postpartum distress.

Hospitalization can be a traumatic event, however, no matter what the precipitating factors. For those who do not fully understand the nature of the treatment, it sometimes has repercussions in terms of the woman's self-concept and may foster a perception of the new mother as being in a permanent "fragile state". Even if hospitalization is not the recourse, just the experience of depression can leave a woman with a similar residue of fears and vulnerability, and an attitude of inability to control her own life and feelings.

Women (and their mates) often attach the experience of this psychological change only to the time of pregnancy itself. In reality, this feeling may hang on for several months (possibly years) after the birth. Physiologically a woman who has just borne a child takes a long time to return to the "pre-pregnancy state." Unfortunately, the dynamics of the woman and her world and the relationships of the couple and extended family do not always return at the same rate, and sometimes not at all.

"I can't seem to shake this feeling. How come I can't get motivated to work when I have so many responsibilities?"

THE CAUSE MAY BE DIFFERENT, BUT FATHERS GET DEPRESSED TOO

Men are also at a precarious stage when they become fathers and take on the responsibilities of a family. For them, depression may be associated with concern about the loss of intimacy with their partner or questions about just how they will fit into this family when so much of new babies seems to have to do with mothers rather than fathers. Knowing that he has now crossed a life threshold and for years to come will very possibly be the major financial support for this group can throw a new father into a state of exhilaration or despair. If it's despair, is it happening because he doesn't love his partner, doesn't want to help care for the family and doesn't want to participate in the experience? Probably not, but these are questions that anyone might raise during a time of such major changes - and the questions just might get expressed as depression. Another facet to the problem is that since so much of others' attention is focused on the new mother, what is happening with fathers can get pushed way to the side. Sometimes people express the attitude, "What does <u>he</u> have to complain about, <u>she's</u> the one who had the baby!"

Women talk about their husbands "just sitting around the house staring at the television for hours on end," or "Leaving to drive around in the car, not coming back until late at night. " These men are telling a story with their actions that they might not be able to tell with their words - they're feeling overwhelmed by their new life roles. They need understanding and support from friends, relatives and their partner as they, too, make the transition from couplehood to parenthood.

"After the baby was born, I couldn't wait to tell everyone I knew about it. I was the proud father. I had been attending LaMaze classes for several weeks with my wife, and I was gung-ho to be a responsible dad. I don't know why it hit me, but a couple of weeks after the birth, I was driving to work and I felt overwhelmed by this sense of anxiety. I felt really scared. That day I went to work, but I couldn't concentrate. When I went home in the evening I felt like I was wading through water. There was Nancy and the baby - doing fine, but I wasn't.

"For the first few days I thought I was getting sick with a virus, but eventually I had to admit that I was making up excuses not to go back to work. The more I put it off, the more scared I became - I watched our income start to dwindle and I kept thinking that I should just leave so that Nancy and the baby could get help from someone else who could really take care of them. This all came about after years of being together as a couple. Plus, I had been in my present job for over five years - was on my way up the ladder and had no <u>real </u>reason to think that I couldn't be the provider for my family, but that didn't stop my mind from going crazy with doubt.

"Finally, after several days of asking me what was wrong, Nancy called her parents and they came over to the house. I was furious at her for calling them and I wanted to hide in the back room just like a kid. Luckily, both her dad and mom sought me out and got me to start talking. At first, I wouldn't tell them that anything was wrong!

"I guess what made the difference was Nancy's dad telling me that he had had the same feelings when he became a father thirty years before. As he talked, I started to see

that it wasn't so unusual to go into a tailspin after becoming a new father. It was the biggest thing that had ever happened to me - I guess I had a right to get a little carried away! He also helped me see that I did have a lot of people behind me and I wasn't alone. Somehow, having someone who had been through it and who didn't think that I was being irresponsible made all the difference."

HARD TIMES FOR OUR FRIENDS AND RELATIVES

Our method of handling life changes and life crises is often based on the reactions that we observed other people in our families having in the past. Some get depressed. You may have known them when they were going through these times, or you may have heard stories. All of this is valuable information in your journey and is helpful to pass on to others.

FILL OUT THE CHART BELOW.

Reflect on the people you have known who have experienced depression.

	Age When Depressed	What precipitated it?	How did others react?
Mother			
Father			
Brother/Sister			
Uncle/Aunt			
Grandmother			
Grandfather			
Son/Daughter			
Friend			

HAVE <u>YOU</u> EVER BEEN DEPRESSED?

REFLECT ON THE FOLLOWING QUESTIONS.

1. Have you ever been depressed yourself? What precipitated it? What did you learn?

2. How did you recover? <u>Did</u> you recover?

3. Did the experience leave you feeling vulnerable? In what way?

4. Did you become more or less understanding of others who are depressed?

5. Do you have methods that you use for avoiding depression? What are they?

6. Do you have personal warning signals that have to do with depression? What are they? Have you ever seen these same warning signals in others?

SHARE YOUR THOUGHTS AND FEELINGS WITH YOUR PARTNER.

SO NOW YOU HAVE A TWO-YEAR OLD AND YOU'RE THINKING ABOUT DIVORCE. . .

Look around you. While you see many families that are working successfully to have happy, healthy lives, you may also notice that many more couples are struggling to keep their family together. Very often these couples happen to have a small child. And very often that child is just over two years of age. What is happening here? What's so magic about the number TWO? Is it merely a coincidence that so many people seem to be breaking up when they have a two-year old child? There are surely many factors at work. We'll consider just a few.

EXPECTATIONS FOR TIME OF PROBLEM RESOLUTION

Men and women in this "new-age" society are running very fast to stay on top of finances and home-buying and career changes, not to mention attempting to have "enlightened" relationships. All of these factors take an immense amount of time and energy. Are our expectations of what we can accomplish in line with the degree of change and effort that a constantly changing environment may require? I think not. In most cases it seems that people are expected to adjust internally (emotionally, psychologically) just as rapidly as the world is changing around them. These expectations do not just come from the outside; they are also put in place by the individuals themselves as they feel that the world is rushing by and they must keep pace with it.

The result is that we often expect problems to be resolved in a hurry, too. Men and women tend to think that if they haven't worked out a problem in a matter of weeks or months (certainly not years!) they're not going to, and it would probably be better for all concerned if they just moved on down the line.

"Now I know what you meant when you said you were afraid your marriage was breaking up. . ."

Friends and family can also promote these expectations for quick solutions as they go through the pain and anxiety of a difficult relationship right along with a couple

181

or new parents. Ideas and encouragement are tossed out at the struggling couple as friends and relatives rally and attempt to give them support as a new family. Eventually these same people can fall prey to the same disillusionments the couple experiences; after a few years they change their tune. The very people who were supportive in the beginning may be clamoring for a resolution to the problem (and the relationship), putting out massive signals that it's time to move on. The messages seem to be that if this could be resolved, it would be, that major incompatibility problems must be lurking here, that far from being committed mates, you may instead be masochists, intent on driving each other crazy!

Jane and Mike lived out this drama with well-intentioned family and friends for over three years before they gave up, moved apart and found new mates. They began by having a series of arguments about jealousy that never came to any satisfactory conclusion. These arguments created tension in their home that led to other conflicts which were dealt with similarly. This couple had little practice in good communication, and had a lot of work to do to "get on the same side" of any of their problem issues.

During the first months, Jane talked to her best friends and her sister and mother about her fights with Mike. They consoled her, and took her side in the arguments. They all felt Mike was unreasonable, and all agreed that he was showing a particularly "ugly" side of his personality in the conflicts.

"Don't give up. The first two years are often really hard for new parents. I went through it too - forty years ago!"

Mike, on the other hand, never talked to anyone about his troubling homelife. He went to work every day, listened to his coworkers trade stories about their girlfriends and wives, but never participated. He felt confused and angry about what was happening at home. He dreaded seeing any of Jane's friends because he knew that she was spending a lot of time "filling them in on the details." He felt blamed and exposed.

That was how the story went for the first two years. It got to be old hat for Jane's family to hear the new installment of what was going on in her relationship with Mike. She loved him, and couldn't imagine leaving him, but she had only negative tales to tell. Mike spent more and more time with his friends, who gradually picked up on his home discord and encouraged him to leave and "show Jane who's boss."

At this point, even with Mike's acquaintances actively lobbying for an end to the relationship, Jane's "suppprt group" felt she and Mike would work things out if they kept with it. But after two years, everyone seemed to get worn out. Both Jane and Mike felt like mere shadows of their former selves. They seldom had fun together, felt more and more alienated in their daily lives, were not coming up with solutions to their problems, and the "support team" changed its tune.

After so long a struggle, Jane's former supporters began to encourage both parties to end the marriage, make plans based on joint custody of their child and continue with their lives - but heading in different directions. They couldn't imagine that a couple with so many disagreements could ever surface on the positive side of this relationship, and everyone was sick and tired of hearing the repetitive tales of woe that these two young people carried with them. In the final analysis, Jane and Mike suffered from their own lack of communication, wore out their friends and family, and gave up on the promise of a life together.

Who can blame two people who are struggling to create a balance among home and work and friends and parenting when they decide to eliminate a stressful relationship that seems to be taking more than it's giving? But is there more to consider? After the birth of a child, especially, is there a transition happening that is natural, yet runs to completion over a matter of years and not months? **Is it appropriate to encourage couples to hang on just a little bit longer, until they make it past that time period when hormones are rearranging their cycles, when physical and sexual energy is returning, when time commitments for a new baby are lessening, when men and women have gained a perspective to use in re-evaulating themselves in the new role of parent, when life has regained a sense of equilibrium and there is time once more to address the subtleties of passion and intimacy that form the basis of the couple relationship.**

MANY MEN AND WOMEN HAVE FOUND RELIEF AND HOPE FROM HEARING THE VERY REAL STORIES OF OTHERS WHO HAVE MOVED PAST THIS TIME OF EMOTIONAL CHALLENGE AND ARE ON THE OTHER SIDE. IF YOU HAVE A STORY OF PROMISE, SHARE IT WITH SOMEONE YOU KNOW.

FIRST OF ALL, EXAMINE THE THEORY OF "COUPLE CRISIS AND THE TWO-YEAR OLD" - IS IT REAL?

notes/thoughts/ideas
talk to. . .
ask about. . .

LIST TEN COUPLES YOU KNOW WHO HAVE CHILDREN (DON'T FORGET TO INCLUDE YOUR OWN PARENTS)

What happened to their couple relationship during the first two or three years of parenting?

Couple	Divorced/Separated	Stayed Together Happily	Stayed Together Unhappily
1.			
2.			
3.			
4.			
5.			
6.			
7.			
8.			
9.			
10.			

What are your conclusions when you read the chart on the preceding page? Is "couple crisis" a real issue for people who have a small child? If you have identified many couples who have experienced this distress, do you know if they felt alone? If many people feel this way, should it be a concern (and an area of support) for friends and family to address?

notes/thoughts/ideas
talk to. . .
ask about. . .

1. **How many of these people ended up seeing separation or divorce as their best solution to couple problems?**

2. **How many arrived at a divorce after years of discord that <u>began</u> during this crucial time period?**

3. **How many of these couples are still together and have found other solutions to couple dilemmas?**

4. **Where are you, as a couple, on this chart?**

5. **What feelings do you have when you see the information on the chart? Do you feel hopeful? distressed? frustrated? cheered? puzzled?**

6. **Do you think that the people you know are the norm in terms of their solutions to new parenting dilemmas? If not, how are they different?**

WHAT KIND OF HELP DO NEW PARENTS NEED?

FINISH THE FOLLOWING SENTENCES.
These suggestions for new parents can be either from your own experience or from observing others.

1. Try to _____

2. Watch out for _____

3. It helps if you _____

4. I wish I had _____

5. It would have helped me to know _____

6. I was surprised to learn _____

7. It's a good idea to _____

8. After they have a baby, couples need to _____

9. It can make a big difference if you _____

10. A lot of people seem to have trouble with _____

11. Don't get too upset about _____

12. Try to compromise when it comes to _____

13. Tell your partner if _____

14. Whatever you do, make the time to _____

15. Get help with _____

186

IDEAS FROM OTHERS

LIST FIVE IDEAS YOU HAVE GOTTEN FROM OTHER NEW PARENTS THAT CAN HELP SMOOTH THE WAY.

Listen closely for the "news" that they got from other parents or from their own family that have been passed down over many generations.

Be especially aware of the "hints" that seem small, yet can make a big difference in the long run in how you relate to each other or reduce parenting stresses.

notes/thoughts/ideas
talk to. . .
ask about. . .

1.

2.

3.

4.

5.

How do you feel when you see these ideas listed?

Was it easier or more difficult to get other people to give you their ideas than you thought it would be?

Was it easier or more difficult for you to <u>ask</u> for these ideas than you thought it would be?

Which of these ideas have you tried? How did they work?

187

LEARNING FROM OUR OWN PARENTS

notes/thoughts/ideas
talk to. . .
ask about. . .

**Ask your own parents (or someone from another generation) for
ideas about relieving parenting stress on a couple.**
Listen closely for the day-to-day hints that can make a year-to-year difference
in the quality of your relationship as a couple.

1.

2.

3.

4.

5.

How do you feel as you write these possibilities down? Which of these can work for you?

ONE THING YOU WILL NOTICE: MANY COUPLES WITH SMALL CHILDREN
ARE LONG ON FRUSTRATION AND PROBLEMS AND SHORT ON HOPE AND
SOLUTIONS. IF YOU HAVE IDEAS AND INSIGHTS AND WAYS THAT YOU
HAVE MANAGED TO MAINTAIN YOUR SENSE OF COUPLE STRENGTH AND
CLOSENESS, SHARE THESE STORIES WITH YOUR FRIENDS AND
ACQUAINTANCES. THEY NEED TO HEAR YOUR STORY, AND THEY WILL
BENEFIT FROM HEARING THE STORIES THAT HAVE BEEN PASSED ON
TO YOU.

MYTH NUMBER SEVEN
I (WE) HAVE ALREADY TALKED ABOUT THIS, TRIED TO FIGURE IT OUT, DONE EVERYTHING. IT'S HOPELESS.

It's an exciting and on-going process to create understanding, trust and intimacy with loved ones, but working out problems in a relationship can be a long-term proposition. Many parts of life require ongoing maintenance, and relationships of love and parenting are no different. Questions and problems that surface and are resolved one week may be replaced by new concerns the next. Did you grow up in a family where "problems" meant fighting and shouting or frozen silence? How are your own attitudes about working things out a result of your family's influence?

1. **List three things that you've <u>thought of</u> but that you haven't <u>tried</u> to solve your current dilemma.**

2. **Ask a friend or a relative for an idea of what to do. Evaluate that idea and use it if it fits for you. If it doesn't, ask someone else.**

3. **Do you know couples who actually sit down and air their grievances and come to mutual resolution and satisfied compromise?**

4. **Are you afraid to see a change for the better in your relationship? If so, why? Have you sabotaged your own efforts by "pretending" to be working on it when you really haven't been?**

5. **What would happen if you tried a solution that your partner has thought of, but you haven't acted on?**

CHAPTER EIGHT

COMPROMISING

LET'S MAKE A DEAL

You and your partner have a "problem" that you are trying to work out. This "problem" could be in any area of your life together. It might involve philosophical disagreements or questions about day-to-day living. Use the following exercises to sort out feelings and attitudes and define possible steps to solution.

notes/thoughts/ideas
talk to. . .
ask about. . .

"STOP! You're both right! What finally worked for us was to agree on a short-term plan just to get moving on a solution."

What is this problem (in <u>your</u> words)?

What would your partner say the problem is?

What feelings come to the surface when you think about this problem?

_____ sadness	_____ hope
_____ anger	_____ puzzlement
_____ depression	_____ fear
_____ loneliness	_____ desperation
_____ discouragement	_____ embarrassment

As you look at the above list, can you think of another time in your life when you had similar feelings - perhaps about another issue or with another person? How is <u>that</u> time affecting how you are now dealing with <u>this</u> problem?

193

DIVIDE YOUR "PROBLEM" INTO FIVE STEPS TO SOLUTION

notes/thoughts/ideas
talk to. . .
ask about. . .

(If you have trouble with this exercise, look at the example on the next page):

1. _____

What will you do?   When will you do it?   What good will it do you?

2. _____

What will you do?   When will you do it?   What good will it do you?

3. _____

What will you do?   When will you do it?   What good will it do you?

4. _____

What will you do?   When will you do it?   What good will it do you?

5. _____

What will you do?   When will you do it?   What good will it do you?

MIKE AND KERRY'S PROBLEM

Mike and Kerry's problem has to do with dividing up childcare duties. Kerry feels that she is always expected to feed, clothe and wash the baby, although Mike is willing to help out if he's asked. Mike feels that Kerry knows the most about these things, so it naturally makes more sense for her to do them. He also says that although he's ready to help, Kerry always takes over and doesn't trust him take care of the baby in his own way.

The Problem: We need to come up with a plan so that Kerry isn't the only one taking care of the baby.

The Breakdown of the Problem into Five Steps to Solution:

1. Next week, we will each talk to three other couples to see how they divide up childcare duties. We'll find out if other people have the same problem and what they've tried to do about it.

2. On Tuesday, we'll spend the evening talking to each other about how our parents took care of the children in our families as we were growing up. We'll make a list of what we did or didn't like. We'll choose three things from the list to try ourselves.

3. We'll draw up two action plans. We will each write down a "perfect" solution. We'll each get a chance to say what we most want to have happen (even if it won't necessarily happen just that way!)

4. We'll have dinner together (alone - we'll get a babysitter) on Friday night and read the plans. We'll be open to slight revisions to make them workable for both of us, although they may not be perfect at this point. We'll actually go out together and have an enjoyable evening and get further ahead on this at the same time.

5. We'll try each plan for two weeks, and at the end of that time we'll talk about whether or not they worked, and come up with a revised plan if we need to. This'll be good for us, because we can use this plan to work on other problems, too, and it will get us talking instead of yelling about taking care of the children.

BARRIERS TO PROBLEM SOLVING

You have the problem defined and you have identified five steps to solution. Now take this "problem" and take another look, because it's time to find the barriers that could prevent you from resolving it.

PERSONAL BARRIERS:

Name the fears, anxieties or bad habits you have that stand in the way of a solution:

1.

2.

3.

When have you had similar feelings that made problem-solving difficult?

What did you learn from that experience that can help you now?

What will you do to overcome these barriers? When will you do it?

196

INTERPERSONAL BARRIERS:

notes/thoughts/ideas
talk to. . .
ask about. . .

What are the investments that your partner or someone else may have in <u>not</u> resolving this conflict? Why would this be uncomfortable or upsetting for them?

1.

2.

3.

When were <u>you</u> the person who was threatened by the possible solving of a problem? What was happening in your life at that time?

What did you learn about yourself that can help you understand how others are feeling now?

What will you do to overcome these barriers? When will you do it?

INFORMATIONAL BARRIERS:

What information are you lacking to get started on a solution? What do you need to know?

1.

2.

Who can you ask for information - who knows something about this "problem?"

1.

2.

Where can you go for information or ideas? What resources are there in your community? Who can tell you?

1.

2.

What can you do to overcome these barriers? When will you do it?

PLANNING AND NEGOTIATING IS AS IMPORTANT IN ISSUES OF COUPLING, MARRIAGE AND PARENTING AS IT IS IN BUSINESS. AIRING YOUR THOUGHTS AND COMING UP WITH ACTION PLANS ARE THE ONLY WAYS THAT BOTH PARTIES CAN UNDERSTAND THE DYNAMICS OF THE SITUATION AND HAVE A CHANCE TO SEE BEYOND THEIR OWN CONCERNS AND DESIRES.

ALWAYS AND NEVER

ALWAYS and NEVER are emotionally laden words. They have the power to turn a conversation into a verbal battleground. When someone accuses you of ALWAYS or NEVER (and doesn't the use of these words seem like an accusation of the most volatile kind?) they are placing you in a category that you won't be able to get out of. From the viewpoint of the partner who flashes ALWAYS and NEVER like neon signs, your behavior has been classified - no arguments will work against this pronouncement, it's a finished issue. From your vantage point , it is probably just the beginning of trying to convince your partner otherwise, or debate until the level of frustration rises until it's obviously time to call it quits.

"I feel so hopeless when you say I'll never learn to talk to you. Do you really believe that?"

Bob and Barbara were experts at the ALWAYS and NEVER game. The house rang with accusations like "You always come home late when we have guests," and "You never wash the dishes," and "You always make commitments with your friends when you know I'll be home early," and "You never put gas in the car ."

Immediately after the message was delivered, the stage was set for at least an hour of bickering back and forth. "Have you forgotten when I arrived early for the dinner with the Gustafson's and you weren't nearly ready? "I washed the dishes for a week straight just last month!" "I never do that - you're always accusing me of spending time with my friends, but what am I supposed to do? Wait around for you?" "Never remember? Then who is it that fixes breakfast everyday and you wolf it down before you run out the door? Is that the same person who never remembers the way you like your toast? Then maybe you'd like to fix it yourself from now on!"

This couple has allowed two explosive words to dominate their conversations. Instead of an accurate appraisal of what each does or doesn't do, and how the other partner is affected by it, Bob and Barbara have made an art of alienation through the use of ALWAYS and NEVER. Afraid of real communication (what would happen if they could actually sit down and resolve some of their questions and differences?), they use words they know are designed to keep

199

them apart. They wish they could comunicate better, and they wish they could restore some of the relaxed nature that was present when they first met. But underneath, they have a lot of anger about unspoken issues and hurt feelings - and they're taking the easy way out when it comes to releasing this anger. Better than labeling the behavior according to the "number of times it happened (or didn't happen)" is to talk about feelings.

TALKING ABOUT YOUR FEELINGS

THE ALWAYS AND NEVER STATEMENT, I FIND MYSELF USING (OR I AM ACCUSED OF USING) IS:

      You always _____.

      You never _____.

Why does this behavior that happens "always" or "never" upset you?

What situation does this remind you of?

Who does this behavior remind you of?

Who do you sound like when you're upset about this issue?

WHEN OTHERS TALK TO YOU

In every couple there are key words that serve to alienate rather than facilitate. What are the phrases, the pronouncements of ALWAYS and NEVER that you find to be particularly offensive? What feelings do you have when your behavior is categorized in this way?

notes/thoughts/ideas
talk to. . .
ask about. . .

ALWAYS AND NEVER STATEMENT	WHO SAYS THIS TO YOU?	HOW DO YOU FEEL WHEN YOU HEAR IT?

WHEN <u>YOU</u> TALK TO OTHERS

ALWAYS AND NEVER STATEMENT	TO WHOM DO YOU SAY THIS?	HOW DO THEY FEEL/ WHAT DO THEY DO WHEN THEY HEAR IT?

HOW TO AVOID USING ALWAYS AND NEVER
AS BATTLE WORDS

1. Practice. Start eliminating them immediately. Break the habit by noticing how often you use these words and what the result is. If you use a form of communication that angers, insults and discounts your partner, you should be prepared to understand (and explain?) why those are the results you desire.

2. Keep track. For issues that come up frequently, try keeping score. Make charts that show how often dishes are washed, the oil is checked in the car, the dog is fed, the in-laws come over for dinner, etc. Use this chart, not as a way to have more ammunition for an ALWAYS and NEVER fight, but as an obervational tool that will allow you both to see the reality of the situation. This chart is not meant to intimidate, it serves as a real-life gauge of issues and situations that may be triggering real-life struggles. Better communication is ALWAYS the goal. Being one-up on your partner NEVER is. Approach this suggestion of "keeping score" with an attitude of cooperation and clarification, not confrontation.

Some examples follow:

THE ISSUE - CLEANING THE TOILET
THE FACTS - A ONE MONTH CHART SHOWS HOW MANY TIMES THE TOILET WAS
CLEANED, AND BY WHOM.

Confrontation: See, I told you that you never clean the toilet. In an entire month, I was always the one who did it!!

Clarification: It's important for me that you notice that in the last month, I was the only one who cleaned the toilet. If this is a shared duty around our house, you need to start getting some marks on the chart for participating. If it's not, we need to redefine our roles here, so we both know what's going on. I don't like nagging you, you don't like hearing it, now what are we going to do about it?

202

THE ISSUE - NOT CALLING WHEN LATE
THE FACTS - A CHART KEPT FOR TWO WEEKS SHOWED HOW OFTEN EACH PERSON
CALLED TO TELL THE OTHER THEY WOULD BE LATE OR PLANS HAD
CHANGED.

Confrontation: Notice that I called you three times last week when I was late? Now who says that I don't call? Don't go telling me that again, cause I'm not going for it!

Clarification: I'd like you to see that in the last week I did call you three times to say that I'd be late. When you think I never call you, it makes you feel bad, so seeing that I really do call should help you feel better. Why do you think you see me as being that inconsiderate? Let's talk about it. I want you to see me trying to be considerate of you, because I am and I do care.

THE ISSUE - DOING HOMEWORK WITH THE KIDS
THE FACTS - A CHART SHOWS ONE MONTH OF HOMEWORK ASSISTANCE DUTIES WITH
THE KIDS

Confrontation: Look at the chart!!! You never help the kids! In the whole month you only sat down with them once and that was when you sprained your ankle and couldn't go out with your friends! I don't want to be the only one who helps them with their homework!

Clarification: I hate to say this, but when I see the chart it's there in black and white that I only helped the kids once all month. It seems like I'm doing it every night, but I guess I'm not. It's something I want to do better - I never realized how lax I was in this category. Next month I'll be doing a lot better and putting in a lot more time with them.

DO ANY OF THESE VERBAL SCENARIOS SOUND FAMILIAR TO YOU?

203

Is the end result of "always" and "never" arguments positive or exhausting in terms of bringing you closer and making you friendlier as partners?

Does it take a "real effort" to say things in a way that will be soothing rather than inflammatory? Why do you think this is?

When you were growing up, were there "always" and "never" statements that were used at your house? What were they? Who used them? To whom were they directed? Did it help or hinder communication in the family?

Ask your friends - what are their "always" and "never" arguments?

Does it help to think of alternative ways of talking about behavior that needs to change or is it upsetting to one or both of you?

SHARING CHILDCARE - PART I
CAREGIVER OR BREADWINNER?

No matter how much you love your child or appreciate the role of parenting, the time and commitment it takes to get it all done "right" can weigh on you and cause subtle resentments. This is especially true if you think that your partner doesn't really understand what it's like to be the primary caregiver. On the other hand, the income-earner may feel burdened by the responsibilities of supporting a family. In many families, the logistics dictate that one parent stays at home to be the primary parent while the other goes out to earn the income. For the parent who stays at home, there may be a strong sense of isolation from spontaneous times and adult companionship. This parent may feel that he or she is losing a sense of personal identity, spending time in a world of scattered tasks and inconsequential baby conversation.

For Arlene, the days went by in a pleasant, although totally unremarkable manner. She loved her new daughter, liked to play with her and care for her, but found that she also wanted to get away, and felt curiously trapped by her situation. She was having a difficult time defining what the problem was. When Sam came home from work, he would tell her about his day attending environmental conferences and writing legislation that would influence thousands of people. She waited for him to ask her what she had done, and at the same time felt that it wasn't really worth talking about.

Over the months Arlene came to feel that Sam didn't value the time she was putting in to take care of their child. Although Sam loved her and the baby, he, indeed, didn't think that their days amounted to much. When Arlene would start to talk about something that had happened in the house, his attention would wander and she would find herself standing in the kitchen with her voice trailing off, feeling humiliated to be grasping for his attention to her not-so-colorful days.

Arlene became angry that Sam was able to leave every day for an exciting job in the city, yet she also wondered if she had changed so much that she, herself, wouldn't have the stamina or the "edge" to take over that role of breadwinner even if it was offered to her.

Thoughts like these can pile on top each other until they are braided into one confused, bitter expression. Parents who are staying at home, overwhelmed by being twenty-four hour caregivers

205

often feel that their job is "lightweight" and not nearly as important as the "real job" of the person who is bringing in the money. By assigning no monetary value to the "at home" parent's work and by paying substitute caregivers at a low rate/wage, society has supported this notion for many years, so it takes a concentrated effort for couples to derive their own sense of what is fair, and what solutions will be workable for them. Coming to grips with perceptions of time spent, and your feelings about both your activities and the time it takes to do them, is a vital step in reducing partnership resentments that may crop up during childcare years.

Jack's job put him in the spotlight. On the surface, he loved his work and was excited about his future. But underneath he was consumed by fears about supporting his wife and children. Jack had been a happy-go-lucky college student, never saving any money he earned, but never caring. Now, he went off to work with a smile, but his stomach was churning as he pushed himself to keep rising up the corporate ladder so that he could be assured of a high enough income to give his family the things they wanted and needed. He was frightened of being eclipsed in the company by 'young blood" and spent more and more hours at the office trying to guarantee his position.

What had started out as a career of choice was turning into a stress-filled nightmare. He never let his wife know any of these feelings, however, as he wanted her to feel secure and taken care of. He was also vaguely aware that she might want to go out and work to supplement the family income if she knew about the stress he felt. He couldn't face the fact that he might have to change his life by becoming more of a caregiver for their children, while at the same time reducing their standard of living. He hadn't been around for the first years of his children's lives and he felt unable to ecome close to them at this stage of the game. He felt trapped.

"Watching a baby is no big deal! I'll just catch five minutes of quiet reading while she's sleeping. Hmmm, didn't I already read this chapter?"

THE ISSUE OF "PRIMARY PARENT VERSUS BREADWINNER" IS HIGHLY CHARGED WITH EMOTION. IT REQUIRES THAT COUPLES TAKE AN INTENSE LOOK AT THEIR OWN EXPECTATIONS AND THEIR ABILITY (OR DESIRE) TO SUPPORT THE GOALS OF THE OTHER PARENT.

What <u>does</u> it mean if you don't want to stay at home and be the primary parent, yet you don't have the income-earning potential of your partner? Does it mean that you're "stuck" in the parent role? Does it mean that you have no leverage because you don't control the purse strings? And what does it mean if your family has gotten used to a certain lifestyle that you have provided, and your partner can't match that lifestyle with his or her income-earning skills? Are you "stuck" forever as the parent who leaves every day to keep the family at its accustomed standard of living?

LOOK AROUND YOU.

ASK PARENTS, FRIENDS, NEIGHBORS AND STRANGERS HOW THEY HAVE COMBINED CHILD CARE AND INCOME-EARNING TO DEVELOP A COOPERATIVE RELATIONSHIP. LEARN FROM THOSE WITH NO SOLUTIONS AS WELL AS THOSE WITH GREAT IDEAS.

For couples who delve into these questions, the rewards are enormous. They gain from acknowledging each partner's concerns and fears and hopes and dreams, and have the opportunity to create a life plan that will give each the chance to blossom as both a parent and an income-earner. This is the time to take advantage of the solutions that your parents and friends and neighbors have developed over the years. Keep an ear open for stories of men and women who have successfully combined careers and parenting and shared these responsibilities.

Think in terms of short-term and long-range solutions. What may be necessary now may change in two years or five years or ten. As a family, you're planning a lifetime of goals and the roles will shift and meander over those years.

USE THE FOLLOWING PAGES TO BEGIN TO TRACK THE FEELINGS AND IDEAS THAT WILL ALLOW YOU AND YOUR PARTNER TO DEVELOP A TRULY COOPERATIVE PARENTING ADVENTURE.

207

COOPERATIVE PARENTING

notes/thoughts/ideas
talk to. . .
ask about. . .

FILL OUT THE FOLLOWING PAGES.
SHARE YOUR RESPONSES WITH YOUR PARTNER.

The best cooperative parenting situation I can imagine is one where:

The best cooperative parenting arrangement that I've ever heard of is:

208

COOPERATING IN THE FUTURE

I imagine that, in future years, I will want to take on:

_____ more of the parenting
_____ less of the parenting
_____ more of the income-earning
_____ less of the income-earning

These events/ changes would <u>allow</u> me to do that:

1.

2.

3.

These events/changes would <u>prevent</u> me from doing that:

1.

2.

3.

<u>When</u> can I imagine being ready to make such a change, if everything was going well?

209

BEING THE 'AT HOME' PARENT

notes/thoughts/ideas
talk to. . .
ask about. . .

When it comes to being the primary caregiver for the family, right now I am doing:

_____ all of it   _____ more than my share

._____ most of it   _____ less than my share

_____ some of it   _____ an equal amount with my partner

_____ none of it

The feelings that I associate with being the "parent" who is taking care of the family's home needs are:

_____ relief   _____ satisfaction   _____ frustration

_____ joy   _____ relaxation   _____ confinement

_____   _____   _____

When it comes to being the "at home parent":

Before we had a child, I thought I would feel _____

Now that we have a child, I feel _____

What surprises me about these feelings is_____

When I imagined being a parent, I always thought that I would have the role of

_____

The hardest part of being the "at home parent" for me is (would be) _____

_____

The easiest part of being the "at home parent" for me is (would be)_____

_____

210

EARNING THE INCOME

When it comes to being the primary income-earner for the family, right now I am doing:

_____ all of it   _____ more than my share
_____ most of it   _____ less than my share
_____ some of it   _____ an equal amount with my partner
_____ none of it

The feelings that I associate with being the parent who is responsible for earning the primary income for the family are:

_____ relief   _____ satisfaction   _____ frustration
_____ joy   _____ relaxation   _____ confinement

Before I became a parent I thought that I would have the following role in earning money for the family _____

Now that I have a child, when it comes to being the main income-earner, I feel

_____

What surprises me about this feeling is _____

_____

The hardest part of being the income earner for me is (would be) _____

_____

The easiest part of being the income earner for me is (would be) _____

_____

211

HELPING EACH OTHER OUT

In my role as caregiver or income-earner, it would help me if my partner would <u>do</u> the following things:

1.

2.

3.

4.

5.

In my role as caregiver or income-earner, I would appreciate it if my partner would <u>say</u> the following things:

1.

2.

3.

4.

5.

SHARE THESE THOUGHTS WITH YOUR PARTNER.

SHARING CHILDCARE - PART II
SOLUTIONS

Every family must come up with its own solutions to sharing of childcare. There are no pat answers to this one. Each couple will have different methods for achieving harmony and even different ideas of what harmony in sharing child care really means.

notes/thoughts/ideas
talk to. . .
ask about. . .

"I've got to find a new babysitter. I've called everybody in town. Why is this __my__ problem?"

Jake and Vanessa went at the problem of sharing child care as an enlightened couple of the eighties. They made their plans before the baby was born - deciding that both would share the tasks on an equal-time basis. Jake participated in the birth, and took a leave of absence from work for two weeks when the new baby came home from the hospital. The plan was that Vanessa would stay home with baby Jason for the first two months and then go back to work part-time, leaving Jason in a bright, sunny daycare center near home. Sounded like a plan made in heaven.

And it was - until one week before it was time for Vanessa to go back to work, when the daycare center closed and the task of finding a new solution became part of Vanessa's job. While trying to juggle the demands of being a working mother, she put off going back to work full-time and spent her "spare" hours calling neighbors and community resource centers to locate another suitable daycare center for Jason. Vanessa assumed that it was her responsibility to make these arrangements if she was to go back to work at all.

Along the way she began resenting the fact that the "daycare debacle" had all fallen on her shoulders. She and Jake would talk at night about what to do, and it always seemed that if she couldn't find the appropriate solution then she would have to make the sacrifice to stay at home. Because Jake was solidly in his job, the possibility that he would take the time to organize the babysitting, or even take a leave of absence while she started back to work was never discussed. There was an unspoken assumption that this approach "just wouldn't make any sense."

213

We can see in the story above that the issue of sharing childcare responsibilities includes not only the "hands-on" particulars such as who is changing the diaper, who is feeding the baby, or who is washing the clothes, but also who is <u>arranging</u> to have these things done, if both parents have commitments elsewhere.

Being a twenty-four-hour-a-day responsible parent is a big job. Many men and women resent their partner assuming that they will cover all loose ends regarding arrangements for their child. Loose ends are a major part of childrearing. The days rarely go as planned. Work is interrupted by illness or teeth-cutting or minor accidents or a need for more attention. The solutions to the question of who takes up the slack at these times gives a true picture of how the couple is cooperating with child care.

It's not easy to challenge traditional ideas of who chooses (or is elected) to care for the child on the "rough" days. It often seems "right and natural" that the mother be available at these times of illness or need for special care. Especially if the mother has been the primary "at home" parent for the first months, the child may only be bonded to the mother, and not adjust easily to anyone else (even the father) taking over childcare duties. It may seem "right" that the main income-earner not miss his or her work for this parenting task. A parent who is self-employed may find the extra tasks falling squarely on his or her shoulders - after all, this line of reasoning may go, their time is their own, they can arrange it any way they desire.

NONE OF THESE OPTIONS IS NECESSARILY WRONG. THEY MAY ALL BE RIGHT - FOR SOME COUPLES. THE GOAL IS TO EXAMINE THE ISSUES WITH ENOUGH TRUTHFULNESS AND CLARITY TO MAKE DECISIONS THAT ARE COOPERATIVE, AND THAT DO NOT ASSUME THAT ONE PARENT'S TIME IS MORE (OR LESS) VALUABLE THAN THE OTHER'S.

What are the solutions to these debates about whose job it is? This is one of the most crucial areas of parenting in which to solicit the ideas of others. The more you throw out the net for creative solutions (and if you are a couple trying to juggle jobs and child care, you need creative solutions!) the better the chance that you will evolve a method that works well for you.

As a place to start, here are some solutions that have helped couples derive a plan for more sharing, more caring, and less resentment when it came to parenting. All of these plans depended on the couples being able to sit down and talk truthfully about their fears and expectations. In few cases

214

did it happen the right way on the first try. Beginning talks often ended in shouting matches and stalemates, but the desire was there (they were, after all, really fighting for their relationship to be sustained during these crucial childcaring years!) and they came back to the drawing board with new variations and new understandings of other couples and each other.

SOLUTION NUMBER ONE -Pat and Jordon's story:

From the beginning, Pat and Jordon agreed on a cooperative plan for raising their daughter. Even before the birth they mapped this out. They decided that it was important to both of them to be intricately involved in all of the decisions and childcare responsibilities that would go with being parents. One of their fears was that their child would rely on Pat, and Jordon would have to fight his way into active parenting as a father. Coming from a family where his father was an ever-present dad, he wanted the same chance to be part of his daughter's life - even the maintenance part.

From the first day that baby Carla came home, they divided up the actual time that they would devote to "maintenance" tasks. Every day there was a plan for who would take the responsibility for answering cries for attention, feeding (Pat was nursing the baby, extracting milk and saving it in a bottle so Jordon could be a "feeder," too), and changing diapers. In the first weeks, they did it on a morning/afternoon schedule, and alternated nights for getting up for baby duties.

This couple had to rearrange their lives and their work schedules to accommodate a shared plan of childcaring. Since they both got up to care for the baby in the night, they looked like zombies for awhile. Since they both had daytime care duties, too, they developed fragmented social and work lives. So, they didn't look too good, and they struggled to get their other jobs accomplished, but they succeeded in their major goal - they both bonded to Carla and she came to depend on both of them as equal parents. When the chips were down, she would turn to the parent who was "on-duty" and allow the "off-duty" parent to proceed with other parts of his or her life.

As Carla grew older, they realized that the morning on/ afternoon off schedule was far too limiting for leading any kind of life beyond being a parent. Both of these people had to work - they had to have more time off, (and more time on) to make those hours worthwhile. The schedule changed to two days on/two days off (conclusion: still too fragmenting; just when you got used to taking care of the baby, it was time to hand her over again). Then it was two weeks on/two weeks off (conclusion: too much time in between; you got out of the habit of being a caregiver, and it took two days to get back in the swing of things). Then it settled in at one week on /one week off for several years. For this couple, it was a good compromise.

215

What were the details of this arrangement that made it work?

1- It was based on both Pat and Jordon recognizing early on that as much as childcare maintenance might conflict with the details of the rest of their lives, there was no way for them both to be contributing parents without sharing these tasks.

2- It relied on both parents developing occupations that allowed them the freedom to be parents during the day as well as in the evening and at night. This didn't happen all at once, but it did evolve over a period of time - they didn't lose their sense of parenting priority while they built their careers.

3- Being the "parent in charge" was never construed to mean that the other parent couldn't help out (or even take over) if they wanted and if their help was requested. What it <u>did</u> mean was that the "off-duty" parent should in no way feel obligated to do these childcare duties -they would be taken care of by the "on-duty" parent. Many times, "off-duty" was asked to babysit for "on-duty" because of conflicting obligations - the key here was that these were requests (just like you would request assistance from any friend) and the other parent felt fine about saying "SURE!" or "Sorry, that won't work for me."

4 - Being the "parent in charge" never meant that this parent was required to be with the child twenty-four hours a day. Rather it meant that this temporary primary parent arranged all babysitting, day care, meals, clothes washing, etc. It meant that the "off-duty" parent could participate or not as he or she saw fit - they could rely on the fact that the details were being taken care of.

5- This arrangement, by necessity, relied on both parents believing that the other was competent (since they had started the cooperation from DAY ONE, they were rather acutely aware that neither of them had had the time to get ahead in the information or experience department!) and that either might be (surely would be) making decisions about child care that would not be exactly the preference of the "off-duty" parent. Solution - grin and bear it. Suggestions were welcomed - they practiced delivering these suggestions in the most non-threatening tones possible - but they were treated as suggestions, not dictates.

SOLUTION NUMBER TWO - Kathleen and John's story:

In Kathleen and John's new family, the roles were defined along income-earning lines. John had a well-paying, satisfying job with a large company. He was gone from 7:00AM to 6:00PM five days a week, and traveled away from home several times a month. Kathleen was interested in staying home and being "mother" to their child. She was in a career transition point when she became pregnant, and being the stay-at-home mom did not conflict with her goals or expectations.

Despite these understandings, after the first year Kathleen began to feel worn out by being the primary parent. Even when John was home, their daughter would rely on Kathleen for comfort ("No, I don't want you, Daddy, I want Mommy!!"), expected Kathleen to fix her snacks, and ran to her if she needed help. John gradually lost his interest in trying to coax Sally to see him as a source of fun and comfort and stepped further into the background. The strain became more evident as Kathleen became more and more knowledgeable about their neighborhood childcare system. When she and John wanted to go out for the evening, she found that the task of finding a babysitter always fell on her (After all, didn't she know who was available, didn't she see these people every day on the street?) Doctor's and dentist's appointments were her domain, too, as was knowing what toy or blanket or book could provide the right sense of security for Sally when she was feeling bad. By default, John was losing his ability to parent.

On the weekends, John meant to spend time with his family, but after working all week, he often wanted to go to some sporting event with his friends. He liked to catch up on projects around the house, but these often involved major construction that usually meant Sally was in the way. On these same weekends, Kathleen found herself sulking and feeling angry. She saw that she had created a situation where she was "the parent" most of the time. She felt guilty asking John to care for Sally because he did work all week long (wasn't that his part of the deal?) and she didn't blame him for not wanting to be around a child that continually asked for her mother instead.

Their solution involved sitting down with time charts (See Chapter Three - Timing) and getting an accurate view of the time they spent at their respective "jobs." For the first time, both Kathleen and John saw that, even though, as his part of the contract, he was at work eleven hours a day (including commuting), indeed Kathleen was on her "job" as parent twenty-two hours a day. When weekends came around, he was off the clock, she was not. So hour for hour, they figured that John was working 55 hours per week, while Kathleen was putting in an average of 168. This included the hours when Sally was sleeping, when only Kathleen would get up if Sally cried during the night or was ill. These figures let them both see the time inequity in a black and white way and they decided it was time to change their parenting roles.

217

What were the details of this arrangement that made it work?

1 - The way they did it was to lay out a new plan on a chart. They decided that if John's job took 55 hours/week, then Kathleen would also be responsible for 55 hours/week at her "job" with Sally. That meant that they had 113 hours per week that fell into the "outside time zone" when they would negotiate for Sally's childcare. They each were to be responsible for 56.5 of those hours, with a flexible scheduling plan that worked around John's trips away from home.

2 - They didn't give up when it didn't work out right off the bat. For instance, it actually took two months of Kathleen reminding Sally that John was taking care of her on "his" hours before Sally started to rely on him for her care. It was necessary for Kathleen to leave on some of the weekends when she would have preferred to be at home, so that John and Sally could spend time alone without her influence on their parent/child relationship.

3 - John had to find new ways to be with his child. During the first two years of her life, he hadn't watched very closely to see just how child care happened on a regular basis. His first instinct was to find babysitters for her so he could go out with his friends. This was hard for Kathleen, who would not have used this solution to gain time for herself, but she sat back to watch the developments as John networked to find a babysitting system in their neighborhood that could work for him. He found out that babysitters wanted at least two days' notice, so he learned to arrange his schedule accordingly.

4 - They learned from each other. Kathleen saw how John used his organizational business techniques to schedule his days - he operated much more efficiently with Sally around than Kathleen did! John asked Kathleen how she smoothed over rough spots with Sally during the day, and he learned from listening to her experience. Kathleen marveled at the way John took Sally on bike rides, riding in a backpack, or took her to the gym while he played racquetball, setting her up with her toys in an adjacent room with a window. She saw for the first time how she had limited her own life and had not been creative enough about getting time for herself.

5- When Sally was sick during the night and it was John's turn to be on "call," Kathleen swallowed her tendency to take over and assume that her sleep was not as important as John's because she didn't go off to a "real job" every day. John grew to appreciate the stress and the joy that child care brings to a parent - he developed an appreciation for Kathleen's efforts that he hadn't had during the first two years of Sally's life.

6 - They traded time back and forth. Now that John an active part of the parenting picture, Kathleen had no resentments about trading time with him and taking Sally when he had something else he wanted to do. She knew that she would be given this same consideration in return. In fact, now that she had free time for herself, she looked forward to spending time with Sally in a way that she hadn't felt since Sally was a small baby.

SOLUTION NUMBER THREE - Jeff and Gerry's story:

After Baby Joshua was born, Jeff and Gerry came up with a childcare solution that set out eighteen years of their life together! They were both long-term planners and felt that they needed to have a series of goals in front of them so that they could each follow their careers and still be parents to Joshua. They felt capable of rolling with the day to day vagaries of parenting, if they could see the ultimate path that they had signed up for.

The overall goals were clear, but neither had much practice in working in a truly cooperative way in any other relationships. They made a plan that was divided into six-year segments. During the first six year phase, Jeff wanted to live where they were currently established. He was given the choice to decide where they would set up their residence, and was designated the person primarily responsible for the income-earning (and they would live according to his income and standard of living) for Phase I. He would have six years to develop his career and work at what he wanted. Gerry was given the second phase of six years, and they decided that Joshua (who was only three months old when this all went down in writing!) would get to have the major input for the last six years, when he would be in junior high and high school.

What were the details of this arrangement that made it work?

1 - They made the commitment to trust each other. They knew that they had to establish   absolute trust that both parties would stick to agreements made years before. They placed their faith in this couple and family relationship and "dug in" for the duration.

2- During Phase I, Gerry would be the primary parent at home, but this would not prevent working and pursuing a career to whatever extent was desired. Jeff would also be expected to participate in the parenting tasks. They knew that this had to be or Jeff would never develop the bonding with Joshua that would enable him to be a successful parent when his time came around.

3 - During Phase II, the roles would reverse, Gerry would choose where they would live (including the possibility of staying where they were already located) and would take on the income-earning duties, making money according to Gerry's own career plans, and the family living according to the accompanying standard of living. Jeff would be the primary parent at home, with the potential to continue his career as he saw fit, and as it fit into the family homelife.

4 - During Phase III, the family would decide as a unit where they would live, with Joshua being given major input since he would be at a vital point in his school years and be attached to friends, etc., and both parents would work or combine parenting. Phase III was structured more loosely, with the understanding that Joshua would not be requiring so much time from an "at-home" parent, each adult could expand their careers while working at being parents together.

219

5- During each phase, the "at home" parent was the figure who would keep the family rolling at home, but the other parent was expected to be taking on shared childcare duties at the same time. This meant that each had a "job" for a six year segment, but the parent at home had a back-up at all times for their efforts. It was not acceptable to be only the income-earner and not be part of the family life at home.

7 - They went into this agreement knowing that Gerry would probably not be able to earn as much money as Jeff when it came time for Gerry's "employment phase" of the relationship. Gerry had limited education and was going to be starting out at a lower salary base. - lower than Jeff's in the first six years. They knew that if this was important to Jeff, he might have to "get ahead" financially for them before Gerry's six years came around, or he would be part of a family living in a more low-key manner in order to accomodate their family goals. Gerry knew there was the option (not the obligation) to get a running start on a career during Jeff's phase, and be well on the way financially and professionally by the time responsibility for the income of the family came around.

SOLUTION NUMBER FOUR - <u>YOUR</u> STORY:

MYTH NUMBER EIGHT
I CAN'T GET ANY COOPERATION

Bad feelings about lack of cooperation have caused many a problem-solving venture to stop dead in its tracks. It is fruitless to try to force cooperation from partners or family members. No matter how much we might like to see their participation, it may be more productive in making major changes to begin the effort ourselves. Partners who may be fearful of change or resolution can often relax when another takes the initiative, and may come to participate fully later on.

notes/thoughts/ideas
talk to. . .
ask about. . .

1. Who was in charge of getting negotiations moving in your family when you were growing up?

2. Did your parents "cooperate" to resolve differences. Give an example.

3. Do you feel that without full participation from your partner you don't want to (or can't) begin trying out solutions? How long will you be willing to have this stance before you take action on your own?

4. Describe how can you move off dead-center in regard to a current dilemma and gain cooperation from your partner.

5. Ask a couple you know how they manage to cooperate in their relationship. Try out one of their ideas.

221

CHAPTER NINE

PLANNING

WHAT'S IMPORTANT TO ME

As we move through the many stages of our lives, our actions are directed by what we determine to be of importance to us. Unfortunately, for many people, it is not so easy to identify what is important. Personal goals and values can get confused with those of society and those of our friends and neighbors. And, even if you have a strong sense of your goals and their level of importance, you may not always have ideas for how to establish priorities to direct your life decisions.

One way to determine what is important is to think in terms of "values." Values are our ideas of what is right or wrong, good or bad, reasonable or unreasonable, necessary or luxurious. Our values are the motivators behind our decisions and help us determine our action priorities. If we can't make a decision about a current issue, it may be because we aren't that clear about the values we are carrying within us.

Michael had an extremely difficult time making decisions. More than one opportunity passed him by while he was shuffling the alternatives. On his best days, he saw himself as a methodical thinker - someone that weighs all of the possibilities before acting. On his worst days, he berated himself for being a plodder - for not making up his mind and for letting the world go on without him.

When Michael was single, the pitfalls of erratic decision-making only affected him. Then he married Joanne and had two small children. He had three people who needed him to clarify his needs and desires and intentions.

Although his family was very concerned with his "wishy-washiness," Michael was more afraid than anyone when he couldn't make up his mind about important issues. He was in a constant state of anxiety over whether to work full-time or go back to school or stay home and be a "househusband" while Joanne worked. The list went on and on. When Michael and Joanne tried to talk about future plans, he felt his panic level rising; the conversation usually ended in a verbal battle.

"I'm coming back because I believe we can work things out. I want us both to talk about what we really want and need."

225

When Michael showed up at an Adult Education class called Getting Organized, he was in a quandary over whether he should be spending his time on such a class. The first night, however, he learned that there were ways not only to get organized with paperwork, but also to order all the parts of his life so they made sense and he could choose among the alternatives offered to him.

One of the first things he realized was that, for years, he had been operating under the impression that if he structured his time and made concrete choices, he would be losing a lot of the"spontaneous" freedom in his life. The Adult Ed instructor was quickly able to point out that, indeed, he was losing far more freedom by his indecisiveness than he ever would by knowing what he wanted and going after it in a direct manner.

That first class was just the beginning for Michael. He put more time into clarifying what was important to him and why, and what hopes and fears were attached to each issue. He shared these meanderings with Joanne, and she told him about her own dreams for the future and where these dreams had gotten their start.

IN THIS ACT OF MEETING ON A MIDDLE GROUND, AND ACHIEVING WHAT IS VALUED BY EACH PARTNER, COMPROMISE CAN LOOK LIKE SACRIFICE AND INSISTENCE ON PERSONAL GOALS CAN BE PERCEIVED AS OUTRIGHT STUBBORNESS AND BULLYING. ACTS OF GIVING AND TAKING ARE FAR EASIER IF YOU HAVE GIVEN SERIOUS THOUGHT TO THE VARIOUS ISSUES THAT CONFRONT MOST COUPLES AND PARENTS, AND HAVE THOUGHT ABOUT THEIR PRIORITY IN <u>YOUR</u> LIFE.

FILL OUT THE CHART ON THE FOLLOWING PAGE.
For each of the statements, assign a rating of from 1 to 5 depending on its
  importance to you.

> **1 - not at all important**
> **2 - a little bit important**
> **3 - of average importance**
> **4 - important**
> **5- extremely important**

Under "source," write down who has most influenced you in terms of this value (e.g. father,
  mother, grandfather, minister, teacher).
Write a few key words to describe what you plan to do because these values are important to you.

MY VALUES - WHAT'S IMPORTANT TO ME

Value	Rating	Source	Because this is important to me, I want to:	notes/thoughts/ideas talk to. . . ask about. . .
Become educated				
Know the right people				
Be religious				
Don't give in				
Put others first				
Never show negativity				
Be tolerant				
Work hard				
Be independent				
Stand up for others				
Be loyal				
Be part of a family				
Own a house/property				
Be adventuresome				
Be honest				

MAJOR CHANGES IN WHAT'S IMPORTANT

notes/thoughts/ideas
talk to. . .
ask about. . .

Major life passages (birth, marriage, illness, etc.) often provoke a change or re-evaluation of "what is important" to us.

Fill out the time line below. Mark the years when you experienced major changes (or possibly clarification) of what was important to you.

10 yrs   20 yrs   30 yrs   40 yrs   50 yrs   60 yrs   70 yrs   80 yrs   90 yrs

REFLECT ON THESE QUESTIONS AND SHARE YOUR THOUGHTS WITH YOUR PARTNER:

1. What was happening in your life during these periods of time?

2. Did the changing view of what was important grow out of happiness or sadness?

3. Was the change in view prompted by an event that happened to someone else (perhaps another's fortune or misfortune)?

4. How are these significant events and time periods <u>still</u> affecting you?

5. Which of these times of change occurred with your present partner? What should your partner know about your feelings in regard to these times?

228

FIVE YEARS AGO, TEN YEARS AGO...

REFLECT ON THE FOLLOWING QUESTIONS AND SHARE YOUR THOUGHTS WITH YOUR PARTNER:

notes/thoughts/ideas
talk to. . .
ask about. . .

1. How have your ideas of what is important to you changed over the years?

2. How would you describe these changes? Do they seem to be signs of greater maturity and self-knowledge? or instability? or confusion? or shifting values? or. . .?

3. Are the same type of issues important to you now that were important five or ten years ago, or when you were a child (i.e. friends and family or career goal or material possessions)?

4. In your family, was it "okay" for people to change their jobs or career goals or relationships?

5. How does the prospect of changing goals or life directions feel to you (i.e. is it exhilarating, or frightening, or calming, or. . .)?

6. How do you feel when you consider the possibility that your partner might change goals and areas of life importance in his/her life?

7. Do you tend to see differences in what is important to different people as confusing or frightening or wrong or interesting or merely different? Where did this attitude come from?

BEFORE I WAS A PARENT/ NOW THAT I'M A PARENT

notes/thoughts/ideas
talk to. . .
ask about. . .

How have your ideas about being a parent changed, now that you are one?

Before I was a parent, these were my priorities:

Now that I'm a parent, these are my priorities:

<u>for myself</u>

1.

2.

3.

<u>for myself:</u>

1.

2.

3.

<u>for my couple relationship</u>

1.

2.

3.

<u>for my couple relationship</u>

1.

2.

3.

<u>for</u> _____

1.

2.

3.

<u>for</u> _____

1.

2.

3.

SHARE YOUR THOUGHTS WITH YOUR PARTNER

WHAT'S IMPORTANT TO US?

As we strive to develop adult partnerships, we run into the additional tangle of having to take into account not only what is important to us, but also what is important to our partner. Especially if you are in your early twenties (or even younger) you may be just getting close to understanding what <u>you</u> want and need. Adding on the responsibility of taking another's life goals into account may seem overwhelming. And, what if your partner is in the same boat as you- just beginning to get a grip on his or her own life scheme?

At thirty-four Sandy has never spent more than five minutes identifying her life priorities. She always explains her decisions by saying in a rather flip manner, "Oh, I don't know why I did that; I guess I just thought it would be fun at the time." Although she knows there is more to her life than this serendipitous philosophy, she has no practice in defining her values and understanding the life choices that go with them. Sandy has been lucky with jobs and has taken opportunities to become better educated and move up the career ladder. She has many friends and is close to her family. So, what's the problem?

The problem is that Sandy has fallen in love and is trying to have an intimate and long-lasting relationship with a man she thinks she wants to marry. She has the idea that it's time for long-term commitments, but without a history of being goal-oriented and planning to reach these goals, she's afraid to build a structure for her future. Furthermore her current partner is uneasy about Sandy's casual manner of relating to her life. While she has always seen her attitude as "loose and spontaneous," he thinks it may be impossible for him to have a serious relationship with someone who doesn't know why she is motivated to work or play or love. He wants to make plans, but can't figure out whether he and Sandy have enough deep, common values to make their dreams a reality.

"We could move to the city, or buy some land or send you to college. All of those things have to do with <u>us</u>."

231

Discovering what is important to you, so you can then go on and create an exciting plan for your future is not a mysterious process. But it does take time to seriously consider what has motivated you in the past and where you would like to be going in the future. The exercises on the following pages are designed to help you think about what is important to you as a couple and as parents. If you have difficulty with these exercises, that in itself is valuable information. It may begin to answer a big question regarding why communication is difficult for you. It may give you a clue concerning why you feel unclear about your life goals or those of your partner. If you and your partner are to work together, you must be able to define what it is you are working for.

THINK ABOUT THIS: AS PARENTS, YOU WILL HAVE DIFFERENT PRIORITIES FROM THOSE YOU WILL HAVE AS A COUPLE. THE HISTORY AND OBSERVATIONS THAT HAVE LED YOU TO CHOOSE EACH OTHER AS COUPLE/PARTNERS MAY ADD UP SLIGHTLY DIFFERENT WHEN YOU CONSIDER WHAT YOU EACH VALUE AS PARENTS.

OBSERVATIONS ABOUT WHAT'S IMPORTANT:

1. What's important to you may not be important to me.

2. What's important to us now may not be important to us later.

3. What's important to you may be important to me for a different reason.

4. Our behavior will often tell us more about what is important to us than our words.

5. If we listen carefully, we understand why and how these issues affect us in different ways.

FILL OUT THE CHARTS ON THE FOLLOWING PAGES

One of these charts deals with your values as a couple, and the other with
    your values as a parent.

For each of the values, assign a rating from 1 to 5 depending on how important
    this value or issue is to you/your partner :

        1 - not at all important
        2 - a little bit important
        3 - of average importance
        4 - important
        5 - extremely important

WHAT'S IMPORTANT TO US <u>AS A COUPLE</u>

Value	Rating	Because this is important, we plan to:	notes/thoughts/ideas talk to. . . ask about. . .
Do better than our parents			
Be religious			
Be productive			
Own a house/property			
Be adventuresome			
Live near relatives			
Have mutual friends			
Save money			
Share child care			
Marriage is forever			
Be truthful			
Be physically healthy			
Work hard			
Be faithful			
Physical appearance			
Shared interests			

WHAT'S IMPORTANT TO US <u>AS PARENTS</u>

Value	Rating	Because this is important, we plan to:
To share child care/share finding child care		
Use outside day care		
Save for child's education		
Live in a "good" neighborhood		
Save money		
Have health insurance		
Choose child's friends		
Share meal preparation		
Spend time with grandparents		
Put child to bed at definite time		
Have child sleep in own room		
Use physical discipline		
Allow child to cry		
Teach educational skills at home		
Have child help with chores		

234

WHAT'S IMPORTANT TO YOU NOW
MAY NOT BE IMPORTANT LATER

FILL OUT THE SPACES BELOW

Put a star next to the items that are still important to you now.

What was important to you in your couple relationships five years ago?

_____   _____   _____

_____   _____   _____

_____   _____   _____

_____   _____   _____

_____   _____   _____

What was important to you in your couple relationships ten years ago?

_____   _____   _____

_____   _____   _____

_____   _____   _____

_____   _____   _____

SHARE YOUR RESPONSES WITH YOUR PARTNER

THE ROAD TO SUCCESS

Being able to define success for yourself is important because when you know what success means to you, you can take the next step to identify what you <u>want</u>, and figure out how you will get it.

Emily and Kurt are two people in love who haven't said out loud (to themselves or to each other) what success means to them. Is this a problem? You might think so if you heard them arguing about the size and price of the house they are buying. Or heard Emily crying because, in her view, people who are successful can afford to go on a major vacation every year, while in Kurt's view, successful people put the extra money in the bank for a rainy day. Emily moved with Kurt to a neighborhood where people commute to a larger city for work. There were no community functions. She didn't think about it at the time, but this spelled trouble for them right from the beginning because Emily's idea of a successful housewife is one who spends the day going to community meetings and participating in local charity drives. In this town, none of those things happen.

Emily and Kurt are also having a baby, yet neither of them could even begin to say what their ideals Are for a child's education, or discipline or manners or. . .

"I need to spell out what I want. I keep latching on to your goals and now I need to figure out my own. For some reason it's scary, but I feel better just saying it out loud."

Lots of people navigate through life by their coattails. They go from relationship to relationship, job to job and home to home without a sense of direction. This approach may get you wherever you're going, but there is great satisfaction in setting your own course and having a picture of what will make you feel good as you go through your life. There is also an added benefit in that if <u>you</u> know your goals, then you can relate them to the people who are important to you. Particularly when you are trying to have a partnership, it clears the way for closeness (and much less confusion) if each party knows what the other is striving for.

IF I HAD SUCCESS. . .

ANSWER THESE QUESTIONS AND SHARE YOUR RESPONSES WITH YOUR PARTNER:

1. If I had financial success, the following events would be happening in my life
(e.g. I would be making $2500 a month, be driving a new car, living in New York City).

2. If I had social success, the following events would be happening in my life
(e.g. I would have my name in the social section of the Sunday paper, I would have two very close friends, I would belong to a writing club).

3. If I had success in my couple/marriage partnership, the following events would be happening in my life *(e.g. Every week I would have one night alone with my partner in a romantic place, I would share cooking with my partner, my partner would ask my advice about his/her life questions).*

4. If I had success in my parenting, the following events would be happening in my life *(e.g. I would spend every weekend on camping trips with my kids, I would be attentive and listen to my children's stories about school).*

238

FEARS THAT GO WITH DREAMS OF SUCCESS

Even though you may desire success in all areas of your life, uncertainties can still trip you up along the way. Acknowledging the fears that you may have about achieving success is a first step in overcoming and clearing them out.

If you can talk to your partner about your fears of success as well as your hopes and needs and dreams, you will create an ally who can help you look for opportunity. This person will be understanding of the fits and starts that accompany every journey to a life goal. Without this information, this same person could give up early, as he or she wonders in amazement why you may be your own worst enemy on certain issues that seem to be vital to your growth.

ANSWER THESE QUESTIONS AND SHARE YOUR RESPONSES WITH YOUR PARTNER:

1. What are your fears of success? (e.g. I'm afraid that I will do better than my parents and they will feel inadequate; I'm afraid of having enough money to do the things I say I want to do)

2. Who else knows what your fears are?

3. Who do you know who shares the same fears?

4. Which fears came from your parents? Which came from your friends? How did these fears affect their lives and keep them from <u>their</u> dreams of success? Did they overcome their fears? How?

239

SUCCESS MEANS DIFFERENT THINGS TO DIFFERENT PEOPLE

notes/thoughts/ideas
talk to. . .
ask about. . .

How you view success depends on your fears, your hopes, your history and the messages you have received from others in your life. This last is especially important, because it is likely that each of these people has also viewed success in quite different ways.

FILL OUT THE FOLLOWING CHART.

What have these message bearers told you about success?

Message bearer	Message about success	What do you think of this message?
Mother		
Father		
Grandmother		
Grandfather		
Brother		
Sister		
Teacher		
Employer		
Minister		
Best Friend		

SHARE YOUR RESPONSES WITH YOUR PARTNER

WORKING TOWARD SUCCESS <u>AS AN INDIVIDUAL</u>

How are you working toward success? What are your plans? What steps are you
   taking to get closer to your goals?

notes/thoughts/ideas
talk to. . .
ask about. . .

STATE A GOAL. Then fill in the boxes with specific steps that you are
   taking or will be taking to reach that goal.
INDICATE THE TIME FRAME THAT YOU HAVE IN MIND FOR EACH STEP
   (e.g.. I am doing Step #1 now, Step #2 will start on January 15, Step #3 will start six
      months later, and Step #4 will start in two years)

MY GOAL IS _____.

step 1

When will you start this step?_____

When will it be completed? _____

step 2

When will you start <u>this</u> step? _____

When will it be completed? _____

step 3

When will you start <u>this</u> step? _____

When will it be completed? _____

step 4

When will you start <u>this</u> step? _____

When will it be completed? _____

SABOTAGING YOUR PARTNER'S SUCCESS

notes/thoughts/ideas
talk to. . .
ask about. . .

WHY IN THE WORLD WOULD ANYONE WANT TO SABOTAGE THEIR PARTNER'S CHANCE FOR SUCCESS?

Success is double-edged business for some people. Along with any fears that you may have about your <u>own</u> success, you may also have considerable misgiving about your partner attaining his or her goals. You don't need to be a cruel and scheming person to subtly work against the goals of people around you. Indeed, you may be fearful that you will be "left in the dust" if your partner's career accelerates, or that you will be left home alone if your mate acquires new friends and learns to socialize. You may even have misgivings about a partner getting counseling for a long-standing problem. Even though you would ideally like to see him or her make life work better, it will mean changes for you too, and this realization could cause subtle resentments. Resentments that aren't understood often lead to anxiety and undermining behavior.

FILL OUT THE FOLLOWING CHART.
How do you feel when you acknowledge these concerns?

Partner's goal that makes you uneasy	How can you avoid sabotaging your partner's efforts?	How can you help your partner succeed?

SHARE YOUR RESPONSES WITH YOUR PARTNER.

WORKING TOWARD SUCCESS <u>AS A COUPLE</u>

Just as you establish goals for your individual dreams, you can (and should) establish goals for your future as a couple.

STATE A GOAL. Then fill in the boxes with the specific steps that, as a couple, you are taking or will be taking to reach that goal.
INDICATE THE TIME FRAME THAT YOU HAVE IN MIND FOR EACH STEP
    (e.g.. we are working on Step 1 now, we will start Step #2 in July of this year, Step 3 we will begin two months later, Step 4 we will start one month after that)

OUR GOAL IS _____ .

step 1

When will you start this step? _____

When will it be completed? _____

step 2

When will you start <u>this</u> step? _____

When will it be completed? _____

step 3

When will you start <u>this</u> step? _____

When will it be completed? _____

step 4

When will you start <u>this</u> step? _____

When will it be completed? _____

243

MYTH NUMBER NINE
I (HE/SHE) ALWAYS GO BACK TO DOING THINGS THE SAME WAY

In all complex life situations, we must acknowledge the fact that while a part of us wants things to change for the better, another part is fighting to maintain the status quo. Our habits, our fears, the models we have followed from friends and family, our angers and our frustrations can all beckon us back to the "old ways." This can happen even if the "old ways" are causing pain and disruption in our lives.

notes/thoughts/ideas
talk to. . .
ask about. . .

1. Do you think that people ever really change?

2. Do you know someone who has made a dramatic change for their (or their partner's) best interest?

3. When in your life did you go back to doing things the same way even though you had decided that you would change?

4. When did you decide to change and actually do so? What made the difference?

5. Have you ever had the feeling that you didn't want to change primarily because other people around you would notice and conclude that you had been wrong all along?

245

CHAPTER TEN

BELIEVING

A LEAP OF FAITH

Working on conflicts in relationships can be a trying business. There are times when the progress is faster than we would have imagined, and times when it is excruciatingly slow. Feelings about "being right" and "not letting go" of major issues can stop progress in the beginning stages and bring negotiations to a halt. Attempts to get back on track resolving the disagreement may start out fine, only to stall and cause more frustration. And, there are times when we feel that we "know we are right" and that our partner must acknowledge this before we can go on.

Frank and Sarah played out the "admit that I'm right" game once too often. Whenever they had an argument, they would demand that the other person recognize the "rightness" of their perspective - or all communication would grind to a nasty standstill. Many years of battling over daily activities and bigger values wore them down and they were ready to move on to another partner and an "easier" relationship. But, just before they made this decision, Sarah became pregnant and they decided to make one last try at holding together their relationship which had begun in high school and continued for over ten years.

Now the stakes were higher than ever. Sarah had a difficult pregnancy, Frank was grappling with changes in work and career. They moved to a new town to be near Sarah's sister, but she then moved to another location within a few months. Sarah and Frank found themselves alone, on opposite sides of almost every issue, and very frightened of what would become of them when the baby was born and they had to start interacting as a family or make choices about which directions the members of the family would go if they split up.

The inevitability of a break-up forced them to decide to get counseling with a professional family therapist. This alternative had been suggested to them many times over the years, but neither of them thought they could afford the time or the money. Now they realized that they had no choice - they either had to get help from a professional or watch their struggling relationship reach its own demise.

The first evening with the therapist made a difference for Sarah and Frank that would smooth out many rough roads in the future. The therapist had them write down the reasons they had gotten together in the first place. Most important, she had both Sarah and Frank define areas of their lives where they were prepared to take a stance of "belief" in the relationship rather than attach themselves to adversarial positions. The therapist gave them no choice - they had to leave the session having taken a "leap of

249

faith" to believe in the rightness of their attraction to each other and the possibility that they could learn to work together. While she reassured them that all problems would be addressed along the way, the most important item on the agenda was to reaffirm their desire to be together and their faith in each other's ability to care about the couple relationship.

Even though Sarah and Frank had been saying "I love you" for years - their actions had denied this statement. They behaved as if they were enemies, fighting to the finish over every issue. Through counseling, they learned to step back, relax and believe in the future. They learned to be perceptive about when it was the "right" time or the "wrong" time to pursue solutions to problems. In the short run, they were giving each other (and themselves) the benefit of the doubt. In the long run,they were able to renew their energy for the relationship and develop hope as a family with their new baby.

There are times when a grandiose leap of faith is important in any human interaction. The leap of faith that you take here will find you consciously recognizing your conflicting feelings and issues, but choosing to bypass them in favor of the end goal in the relationship - the healing of emotions that become ragged during conflict. Skipping past unfinished business would **never** be recommended on a regular basis. If this were the foundation of your attempts at conflict resolution, you would be forever dealing with the angers and frustrations that come from pushing feelings down, only to see them rise again to the surface, often in a nastier form.

"I'm glad we decided to spend some time alone, just running in the park. As much as I want to get these things settled, I know we're both getting worn down trying to figure it all out."

EVERY SO OFTEN, INSTEAD OF DELVING INTO EVERY ASPECT OF THE CONFLICT, INSTEAD OF DEMANDING A RESOLUTION RIGHT <u>THEN</u>, TRY SAYING:

This time I won't be so concerned about working out all the details of an agreement.

This time I won't worry about being being right or being understood.

This time I won't be concerned with my anger or bitterness or confusion.

I know that I can address these problems and feelings later, when emotions have cooled down and we are more able to talk.

This time, I will choose to bypass the obstacles and remember what we are trying to achieve as an end goal - to be intimate partners.

I will put out this message to myself and my partner and take a "leap of faith".

I know that my other concerns and feelings will be acknowledged and dealt with at a later time.

SAY YES TO BELIEVING IN THE VIABILITY OF YOUR COUPLE RELATIONSHIP.

251

TAKING A LEAP OF FAITH

notes/thoughts/ideas
talk to. . .
ask about. . .

Take a conflict or disagreement that has stymied you and your partner. Identify the issues and feelings that would ordinarily demand your attention. What would you have to do to take a "leap of faith" and emphasize your end goal <u>before</u> you work out these important details?

The conflict is _____

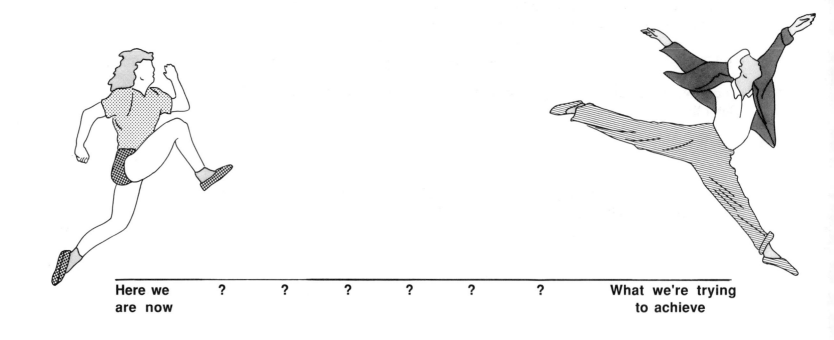

Here we   ?   ?   ?   ?   ?   ?   What we're trying
are now   to achieve

252

THE IDEAL FAMILY

Is there a perfect way for a family to be? There is for you and there is for your partner. But you're lucky (and probably unusual) if you both have the same definition of perfection. For many people, family life goals are so deeply embedded it seems they would obviously be true for anyone who cared to look. Not so.

Carole and Jeffrey got along in most ways. They went on trips together, had many friends in common and both worked in the field of dentistry. Their problems arose because they had very different ideas about the family "meal time".

Carole grew up in a household where mealtime was bedlam and everyone tried to eat as fast as possible. Even with five kids, Carole's mother did all of the cooking. Their father came home from work, was pleasant but never talkative, and the family drifted in to eat whenever they felt like it. There were often battles at the table, both verbal and physical, between her brothers and sisters. Over the years, mealtime turned into an arena of anxiety for Carole.

Jeffrey's family was a bit different, though not the opposite by any means. He had one brother, and both of the boys were involved in school sports. Jeffrey's mother prepared the meals and had dinner on the table to be eaten whenever they came home. Their father would arrive later and have dinner with their mother while the boys were out with their friends. It was a low-key family scene, without much real contact among the family members.

The ways in which you saw family life being created while you were young will provide strong models for you as an adult. These ideas may inspire you to create your new family structure in the same way, or drive you to

"I always thought we'd belong to a country club and have your parents over for dinner on Sunday nights - like my family did. You don't like those ideas, huh?"

253

paint a family picture that is quite different from that of your childhood. And, of course, as a couple striving to have a "couple" partnership as well as a "family" you will have to take into account the expectations of your partner as well as yourself.

When they were living together, Jeffrey and Carole talked about the differences in their growing up experiences, and the discussions stayed on an even keel. Once they had a family of their own, however, Carole found that she wanted their family dinners to be opposite of those she was raised with. She wanted to have a set time for dinner, have Jeffrey participate in the preparation of the meals with her, and sit down at the table like a "real family." Jeffrey, on the other hand, thought that "a real family" could casually walk in and eat whenever the members wanted, that the wife would cook the meals, and if she didn't want to, they could go out. He didn't see any reason for all the fuss.

As time went by, Carole found herself experiencing a deep sadness over this dilemma. She felt that she was a failure in creating the kind of family that she valued in others' lives and that she wanted for herself and her child. Jeffrey and Carole began to have some ugly confrontations over this issue, and they had a difficult time coming up with solutions. They were chafing at the very core of their personal histories on what is a central theme in many family lives - what to do at mealtime.

Knowing the stuff of your dreams for the "ideal family" is important for both you and your partner. Explore these ideas, even if you feel they are impossible goals or your partner has not indicated the ability or interest (up to this point) to help you realize those goals.

Because family feelings run deep, it is essential to learn to listen with care and with a commitment to helping each other achieve "family life goals" whenever possible. Of course, your goals may directly conflict with those of your partner! Then it's time to learn from others. It's time to put out the net for ideas and solutions, as this is one problem that you may back off from, but it won't go away.

NEVER SLIGHT OR BELITTLE YOUR DESIRES OR THOSE OF YOUR PARTNER FOR A "TRUE FAMILY," FOR WE ALL HAVE SUCH HOPES AND EXPECTATIONS AND THEY RUN DEEP - THEY ARE SOME OF OUR MOST POWERFUL LIFE DREAMS.

WHAT HAPPENS IN THE "IDEAL" FAMILY?

FILL OUT THE FOLLOWING CHART WITH YOUR IDEAS FOR WHAT HAPPENS IN THE "IDEAL FAMILY."

How have your ideas changed now that you have become a parent?

notes/thoughts/ideas
talk to. . .
ask about. . .

| | Before I had a child | | Now that I have a child | |
	men	women	men	women
Who's the boss?				
Who takes care of the children?				
Who fixes the meals?				
Who cleans the house?				
Who does the outside work?				
Who's the disciplinarian?				
Who makes the money?				
Who spends the money?				
Who makes the decisions?				
Who's the most affectionate?				
Who gets angry?				
Who gives in?				

SHARE YOUR RESPONSES WITH YOUR PARTNER

255

REFLECT ON THE FOLLOWING QUESTIONS:

1. How did you view these family tasks when you were single? Now that you are married? If your views changed, what do you think caused that change?

2. What is the traditional view of couples and marriage and parenting tasks in your family or your family's cultural history? How would your parents have filled out the chart?

3. In your family, which were the issues with the strongest feelings attached to them - the ones where everyone knew just what was acceptable and what wasn't? Are you striving to make these areas happen the same or differently in your own family?

4. Which of these issues make you feel very uncomfortable to think about doing any other way than what "feels right" for you?

5. What events or situations do these "hot" issues remind you of? Do they bring back memories from your own childhood and from watching your parents live out their ideas of the "perfect" family?

6. Did your parents have an easy or difficult time with expectations around family life? How did their experience (and yours growing up in the family) influence the way you feel today about working things out with your partner? Do you feel hopeful or helpless?

7. Which issues are "trade-offs" - ones on which you feel fairly flexible. These probably do not create a strong emotional response.

SPENDING TIME WITH YOUR "IDEAL" FAMILY

How many people are there in your "ideal" family?

notes/thoughts/ideas
talk to. . .
ask about. . .

Where does this family live?

What happens at mealtime?

What happens at bedtime? With the children? With the parents?

What are weekends like?

What does this family do on vacations? Where do they go?

PUT STARS NEXT TO THE ITEMS THAT FEEL CRUCIAL TO YOU. These
are the items that tell you that "A family just isn't a family unless. . ."

SHARE YOUR THOUGHTS WITH YOUR PARTNER.

THE "IDEAL' FAMILY AND THE FAMILY I GREW UP IN

notes/thoughts/ideas
talk to. . .
ask about. . .

How is your "ideal" family the same or different from the one you grew up in?

In these ways my ideals and my family are the same:

In these ways my ideals and my family are different:

List three things that your partner could do to make your family life come closer to your ideals:

1.

2.

3.

What fears do you have that this might actually happen?

What three things can you do to help your partner achieve his or her family goals?

1.

2.

3.

258

SHARED DREAMS; SHARE

᷐OR IDEAL FAMILIES

What ideals and goals do you and your partner <u>share</u> for your family?

notes/thoughts/ideas
talk to. . .
ask about. . .

1.

2.

3.

Sometimes your family and friends do not share with you your same ideals for
family life. List the people you know who <u>can</u> support you in your quest for a
"real family" because they care about the same issues and are striving for the
same end result in <u>their</u> family.

1.

2.

3.

4.

5.

259

THE TURNING POINT

THE BELIEF IN A LIFE TURNING POINT HAS BEEN A POWERFUL MOTIVATOR FOR MANY PEOPLE. TO BELIEVE IN A "TURNING POINT" IS TO EXPRESS HOPE FOR THE FUTURE, AND FAITH IN YOUR ABILITY TO OVERCOME PRESENT OBSTACLES AND TO ACHIEVE WHAT IS IMPORTANT TO YOU.

notes/thoughts/ideas
talk to. . .
ask about. . .

Think about the other people in your life who are important to you. What do you know about their turning points?

1. What were the times that seemed to be "turning points" for people you know? Did you ever hear them described as "turning points?"

2. Did their lives change for the better? How?

3. Have you ever talked to them about it?

4. Do you know if their friends and family played an important role in this new direction? What role did <u>you</u> play, if any?

5. Have you seen a "major turn around" for the better in the marriage or couple relationship of someone you know?

6. What precipitated this "turning point?" Did you ever talk to the couple about it?

IMAGING THE FUTURE

notes/thoughts/ideas
talk to. . .
ask about. . .

**Do the exercises on the following pages when you have plenty of
time and a quiet place to relax.**

Read the following directions very slowly and think very carefully about the
images that come to mind. Let your imagination carry you back and forth in
time.

Picture yourself thirty years in the future.
Imagine how you look, what you are wearing, who you are with.
You have achieved your goals in terms of your career, your family
   and your personal relationships.
You are feeling happy with the direction your life has taken.
You have reached a point of self-satisfaction and self-acceptance.

Now, as you stand at that point in the future, see yourself turning
   around very, very slowly, You are looking back to this week,
   and you are saying to yourself:

"Ah, I would have never guessed it at the time, but that
week was the Turning Point in my life. That was the
week when everything started to get so much better. . ."

THE LIFE TIME LINE

If you can imagine yourself thirty years in the future,
And can imagine looking backwards to the present,
You can also imagine what happened in those years in between.
And, if you can imagine what happened in between to be happy and
 successful,
You know where to begin.

Take the images that you brought to mind on the previous page and use them
 when you label the time line below. Write in the years of your life, events,
 feelings, thoughts and transitions. (e.g. now I am 28, at 35 I started a savings account,
 at 37 I went back to college and joined a community family support group, at 40 I got my degree
 and started to teach. . .)

Now   **In the future**

LOOK AT YOUR TURNING POINT TIME LINE AND REFLECT ON THE FOLLOWING QUESTIONS. SHARE YOUR THOUGHTS WITH YOUR PARTNER.

Over the span of thirty years on the time line:

1. What happened to you along the way?

2. Who helped you? Whom did you ask for advice?

3. What were the barriers that you overcame?

4. What were the highlights of your journey?

5. What gave you the greatest joy and satisfaction?

6. What did you learn to understand and appreciate about your partner?

7. How did your work and career change and develop?

8. What did you learn?

9. Whom did you love?

10. What did someone teach you that made a difference?

11. What did you learn to understand and appreciate about yourself?

12. How were you able to help others along the way?

IS THIS WEEK THE TIME OF YOUR TURNING POINT FOR YOUR COUPLE RELATIONSHIP? IS THIS THE BEGINNING WHEN EVERYTHING STARTS TO GET SO MUCH EASIER AND SO MUCH CLEARER?

MYTH NUMBER TEN
THIS TIME OF TRANSITION WILL NEVER END

notes/thoughts/ideas
talk to. . .
ask about. . .

When you're in the middle of a transition, or even near the finish, one of the most common things to feel is that "it will never end." Especially if this time of change is stressful and confusing, it may seem like the new set of rules and behaviors has taken over, and the "old life" has fallen far by the wayside. For most new parents, the difficulties of the transition time that includes pregnancy and childrearing of a toddler do end. But, most parents find that it takes a few years - usually two to three. And during that period of time tempers get short, issues get complex, feelings get detached and commitments get brought back for review. Just about the time when many people are giving up on their couple relationship, it's time for feelings and lives to calm down and begin again with renewed energy. This is all fine and dandy, if you've managed to be one of the lucky couples who've held on and haven't been too bruised by a difficult time of change. I believe just knowing that this transition is natural and is difficult, yet has it's termination point can give a sense of hope and future to men and women who might otherwise doubt their options as a couple.

1. **Can you see, in your relationship, the common beginning points of the parenthood transition?**

2. **Have you felt during this period of time that you've seen evidence of the "worst" in yourself or your partner? If so, can you believe this is the exception, not the rule - that this may very well be the one of the lowpoints of your life in terms of your ability to cope with stress and the demands of a whole new role? - and that it is a transition time rather than a "new state" of mind?**

3. **Do you believe that this may be one of the high points in your life in terms of the information you will gain about each other, and the opportunity it will provide for you to be closer and give support and encouragement to your new family?**

CONCLUSION

The goal of TROUBLE IN PARADISE has been to encourage you and your partner to sit down and work together to understand the dynamics of pregnancy, childbirth and parenting and see how they may be affecting your couple relationship. When faced with difficulties after the birth of a child, the "most natural response" is not always to relax and separate out the issues and the feelings. It can be very difficult to work your way through a field of knowledge and communication, searching for your own answers, especially when you have two full time jobs on your hands - being a couple and being a parent. I know it is difficult because I went through the process myself and I have talked to hundreds of other men and women who have been looking for similar clues, similar answers.

Having the interest and the courage to examine personal and family histories and consider how these backgrounds have affected you as an individual, a couple and as a parent is an important step. A crucial tool of this understanding is the information you gain from others who have reflected on similar situations, perhaps in their own lives. The exchange of "news" and support between friends, parents and even strangers about this wonderful and trying life passage can be a lifeline for those who have run short of ideas and are still a long way from being settled as a couple and as a family. For those who choose to pass on their experiences and insights, it is an opportunity to affirm personal growth and integrity over many years of living. It is a chance to give precious clues to friends and loved ones and children who will follow - seeking their own answers and asking their own questions.

While reading TROUBLE IN PARADISE and working on the exercises, did you think of issues and feelings differently? Did you see your partner (or yourself) in a new light that made conflicts easier to deal with and less volatile? Did you feel relaxed and questioning? Did you talk? Did you listen? Did you ask people who are older and younger for their perspectives on being a couple and a parent? Did you talk to your own parents? Did you learn something new? Will you pass it on to others?

I would like to know how this book worked for you. If you would like to share your questions and answers and stories, please send them to the author in care of Dry Creek Press, PO BOX 2037, Napa, California 94558.

267

Order Form

Dry Creek Press
PO Box 2037
Napa, California 94558
(707) 226-7342

TROUBLE IN PARADISE: A SURVIVAL GUIDE FOR COUPLES WHO ARE PARENTS

Please send _____ **copies to:**

Name: _____

Address: _____

City: _____ State: _____ Zip: _____

Yes, I would like to send a copy to a friend at the following address:

1) Name: _____

Address: _____

City: _____ State:_____ Zip: _____

2) Name: _____

Address: _____

City: _____ State: _____ Zip: _____

3) Name: _____

Address: _____

City: _____ State: _____ Zip: _____

Total number of copies ordered _____ @ 16.95 each = _____

Californians: Please add 6% sales tax ($1.02/book) _____

Shipping: Enclose $1.00 per book. _____

TOTAL (check, money order) $ _____